Whole Person Drumming

Your Journey into Rhythm

Zorina Wolf

Publishing-Partners

Publishing-Partners
books@Publishing-Partners.com
www.publishing-partners.com

Copyright © 2016 Zorina Wolf
All rights reserved. No part of this book may be reproduced, stored in, introduced into a retrieval system, or transmitted in any form, or by any means (electronic, mechanical, photocopying, recording, or otherwise) without the prior written permission of the publisher except by a reviewer who may quote brief passages in a review.

Printed in the United States of America

Library of Congress Control Number: 2015956435
ISBN: 978-0-9862830-5-5
eISBN: 978-0-9862830-6-2

Editor: Molly Hollenbach
Cover design: Nigel French
Interior design: Marsha Slomowitz
eBook: Marcia Breece

Village Heartbeat® and Design is a registered trademark of B. Zorina Wolf
Whole Person Drumming® is a registered trademark of B. Zorina Wolf

To order copies of Whole Person Drumming, please contact
books@publishing-partners.com

Please visit: www.VillageHeartbeat.com

Free lessons are available at www.WholePersonDrummingBook.com (Free Instruction Videos)
Additional videos accompanying this book are available for purchase at
www.WholePersonDrummingBook.com (Purchase Digital DVD)

First there is a mountain,
Then there is no mountain,
Then there is.

Table of Contents

Introduction	vi
Foreword	vii
Pronunciation Guide	ix
Babatunde Olatunji— My Teacher and Inspiration	xi

one | Getting Started

The Principles of Drumming	1
Why Drum?	3
How to Choose Your Drum	4
Drum Care	5
Drum Language and Basic Techniques	7
Playing with Flow	8
Unit Box Notation	9
Rhythm Syllables	11

two | Learning the Basics

Drumming Warm-Ups	3
Rhythmic Structures	16
Learning Rhythms	18
Finding the 4/4 Groove in the Body	22
Learning Styles	25
How to Practice with the Drum	27
Drumming Classes vs. Solo Work	30

three | Path and Practice

Beginning Practice, Beginning Rhythms	33
Singing and Playing the Drum	36
Two Becomes Three (the Cross Pattern)	38
Baba's Rhythmic Patterns	41
In YOUR Body!	44
Dance and Drum	46
Developing Focus	47
Always Switch Parts	48
Play with the Other Hand	49
Shifting Awareness Away from the *One*	51
Finding the Elements of Three	51
Single and Double Time Exercises	53
Increase Your Speed and Stamina	55

four | Rhythms That Rock!

Root Rhythms	57
Fanga	60
Baya and Intervals of Four	60
The Bell Rules	63
Cross Rhythms or Two Ways	65
Additive Structured Eight Baya, Top Part	66
The Break	68
Fadeout	71
Rock Rhythm	72
Samba	73
Kpanlogo	76
Sing Three Against Two	78
Complex Body Games in Four	81

five | Further Meditations

Drum Circles	83
Storytelling	85
Visualization for Chi Drumming	86
Play the Parts that Support the Rhythm	89
Competition	90
Sleeping and Rhythm	92
Solar and Lunar Drumming	93
Building the Container— The Art of Mastery	95 / 98
Interviews	100
Glossary	129
Resources	132
Acknowledgements and Thanks	134

Introduction
To My Students and Readers

Hey everyone,

This book has been thought of, dreamed about, agonized about, forgotten about, and now…here it is.

I am a fortunate person. I followed my heart and twenty-five years ago it led me to drumming and rhythm. As I get older, group percussion is still the most bang for my buck. Drumming and rhythm have brought me together with people of all ages, backgrounds, and points of view in a heartfelt way. When we play and listen to one another we are equally important, necessary, and safe with each other. I get to see a village heartbeat evolve in class after class, year after year, and it is still major magic.

I wrote this book for anyone who wants to learn in my style, or anyone who wants to teach in my style, lots or a little.

May this information serve you in learning about yourself, your music and your passion.

Ase,
and Love,
Zorina

Foreword

Hello My Friends,

Zorina Wolf and I have known each other since we were early Babatunde Olatunji devotees and supporters. I can honestly say that over many years, I have watched her grow into the elderhood that she now carries and uses with grace, beauty and humility.

When I first met Zorina, I held her hand and helped her move forward on this path. In the middle of our journey we were walking our talk together side by side, hand in hand. Now with this book, Zorina Wolf is holding my hand and pulling me even further forward on this path.

She sent an advance review copy of *Whole Person Drumming: Your Journey into Rhythm* for me to look over. I couldn't put it down. I had to start at the beginning and read every word, and now I'm going to start the book all over again with a drum in my lap and do all the exercises that are progressively peppered throughout the book.

It's not just an exercise book to introduce beginning drummers to rhythm and playing technique (although it does that elegantly and efficiently). Nor is it just a rhythm journey for an experienced rhythmist who appreciates the deeper, esoteric elements of drumming (although it accomplishes that, too). And it is not just about drumming, but also the discovery, exploration, and integration of rhythms in the world around us. This book will be educational and inspiring to all who take the journey, from the curious beginner to the master drummer.

In *Whole Person Drumming*, Zorina expresses Baba Olatunji's message, philosophy, and mission so well, with Baba's words as well as her own. But more than that, she guides you through the same kind of universal experience and understanding of the power of drumming that Baba would have given you, had you been privileged to work and play with him when he was alive. Baba would be proud.

Life is a dance.
— Arthur Hull

Arthur Hull *is an internationally renowned percussionist,*
and the father of facilitated community drum circles.
Author of Drum Circle Facilitation
http://villagemusiccircles.com/arthurs-corner

Pronunciation Guide

Drum names and drumming terms come from many different languages, and English spelling often doesn't match the sound very well.

Speak a long "u" for the basic drum note, *Gun*, which is always pronounced "goon."

Speak long vowels for the other notes: *go do pa ta* = goh doh pah tah.

Similarly, the *TaKeTiNa* syllables are tah-kay-tee-nah.

For the songs I made up, and for all the wonderful words from Ghana, Brazil, and other parts of the world—don't worry, just wing it! The main thing is the rhythm.

Babatunde Olatunji— My Teacher and Inspiration

How I Met Baba Olatunji and Became a Drummer

In 1960, when I was ten years old, I first saw and heard the great Nigerian drummer, Babatunde Olatunji. He and two other drummers came to my grade school in Baldwin, New York for a cultural enrichment assembly.

Listening to the rhythms of the drums and the energy of the people playing and singing transported me to a state of bliss. I was mesmerized. Thrilled to my ten-year-old core. I was in love.

I went home, convinced my parents to buy Baba's first album, *Drums of Passion*, and told them that I wanted to learn to drum. They bought the album, bought me a set of kiddie plastic bongos, let me loose, and shelved the topic. No one on Long Island was drumming, let alone had a clue what had turned me on. However, the seed was planted. Decades later, this moment came full circle: Baba would become my drum teacher and then my mentor, spiritual guide, and friend.

As I traveled on my life path I tried on lots of different hats: I studied dance, played guitar and sang the blues. I read Tarot cards at the Renaissance Faire. I got involved in acting. I learned to become an esthetician and masseuse, owned and operated a facial salon, got married and had a child. I was an artist, a healer.

In 1988, many life-chapters later, I arrived at Esalen for a bodywork training, and there in the lodge where we ate our meals was Baba Olatunji! It was twenty-nine years since I'd first seen him. He was at Esalen teaching a children's drum and dance camp. This man, who had astonished me in my childhood with his incredible voice and passionate drumming, was right in front of me!

Dressed in a colorful dashiki top and a kufi hat, Baba looked every bit like African royalty. Shivering with excitement, I told him how much his music meant to me and how he had influenced my life. Baba smiled. He remembered the school tour on Long Island. He invited me to sit and have breakfast with him.

Baba asked about my life and what I was learning at Esalen. He asked if I had ever played a drum. "No," I said, "But I've always wanted to."

"Come to my workshop in March," he said.

His invitation was a powerful one—life-changing. Here was my opportunity to reconnect with the music and the man who had touched my heart and soul.

I went. I thought it would be easy and fun to learn Baba's way of drumming and dancing. I wouldn't be as good as he was, of course. I didn't share his deep cultural roots. But I'd be good. Good enough. Piece of cake.

I was wrong. I sucked. By the second day I'd had it. I went to Baba and told him I was going to leave.

"Come to class today," he said. "We will break everything down for you to learn. It will get easier."

But it didn't get easier. What was easy for him was foreign to me. The precision of being with the beat eluded me.

And then there was the dancing. I'd studied ballet. I knew turning out at the hips, five positions, and *port des bras*. I could dance my ass off at rock concerts. But I couldn't get his kind of dance. Isolations? Feet and hip and rib cage and shoulder and head all doing different things? Every part of my body was hurting. And so was every part of my being.

But then there was one amazing moment. After floundering for four days, for one amazing, timeless moment, I fell into rhythm. There was no effort. The drum was playing me! My mind was still and empty of thought. Everything was just happening. I was in the groove!

Once you've touched that place in yourself, a place that is totally in the flow, the heart of all, something calls you forward to find it again and again: to reconnect to movement and stillness. I'd touched that place. I'd felt that call. I was hooked.

The workshop concluded, and at the end of the last day I got on the road around 3 p.m., tearfully leaving my beautiful Big Sur haven. Between the sound of the ocean waves and the feeling in my body, I was swimming in the sensuality of movement.

I started down Highway 1, loving everything about the ride, and noticed that there were some cars piling up behind me. *Well, I'll just pull over and let them pass.* I did that, got back on the road, but very soon I had to pull over again to let the cars go by. The third time, I looked down at my speedometer and realized that although I thought I was zipping down the road, in fact I was driving about eight miles an hour. I had no idea I was going so slow. I was deep in an altered state. After stopping and walking around a bit I felt grounded enough to tackle the highway again.

When I returned home from that first drum workshop with Baba in March of 1989, I realized that something big had shifted inside of me.

I was ready to find or create the kind of beauty and sense of community that I felt at Esalen. I had an idealized picture of the community that could be birthed from people drumming together. My soul flamed with a feeling that we could become a tribe of humans who lived and created together and loved each other. It might have been a flashback from the sixties, but it definitely carried me into beginning to build a large and sustaining drum community.

Drum Community

It's not like I had to create a drum community from scratch; there were already small pockets of people drumming together. I invited anybody I could find to get together to play the drums, whether they knew how or not. Out of those encounters we began to know each other, to build connections. I had a once-a-month drum circle at the Masonic Temple in Menlo Park. I went from the computer geeks in Silicon Valley to the black community across the bridge in East Palo Alto. It was challenging and totally exciting!

About six months into it, I was whacking away in drummer bliss at the drum circle, feeling so proud of myself and my drum family. I was finally a member of a tribe! I had men who were my brothers. They had my back. My yang energy was buzzing and I was flying high on sound, movement and energy.

Then something really strange happened. I heard myself, and realized that I sounded like crap.

It was a pivotal moment, because up to that point I thought I was so cool, so groovy, so completely talented—so YES!

But there was another thing: not only did I sound like crap, but so did everyone else! This "aha" was an important part of my becoming serious about the art and craft of drumming. Unfortunately, it also made it extremely difficult to go back into the bang-a-drum school of hippie-thunder-drumming-random-music without curling my lip in disdain.

More Study

I got serious. I began to attend classes with other teachers, sometimes going to Oakland or Santa Cruz, the two nearest meccas for drummers. I began to practice at home, whether my neighbors liked it or not. I practiced at the park, where my friends could hear me—up to a mile away. I learned about different drumming styles and their complexity: the West African Guinean, Senegalese and Malian *djembe*, the Congolese *ngoma*, the Ghanaian *kpanlogo* drums, the Caribbean groove with conga drums, Brazilian instruments (whew!) *surdo, pandeiro, atabaques, berimbau*, as well as Baba's home roots of Nigeria. I was swimming in rhythm every day and trying to absorb as much as I could, as quickly as I could! Remember: I was forty years old when

I began this exploration, with a three-year-old son.

My journey was arduous. I wanted to learn and master the mechanics of these instruments. I learned to remember rhythms. I made connections to interlink instrumental technique with rhythm to produce music. I trained my body to respond to the beat of the drum. I learned a new way to dance. I sang from my spirit, not my trained voice. I organized drum events—drum circles, solstice gatherings—any excuse to drum with other people.

After two years, I formed a drum and dance band. We were all students of the drum who wanted to share our passion with the world. I named the group Village Heartbeat®. We performed for events at schools, libraries, arts centers, and festivals. We became known as community performers in the San Francisco Bay Area.

Learning in Public

I loved Baba fiercely. Baba was my ticket to joy! Twice a year, I committed time to be with him at Esalen. These annual events in spring and summer were mandatory for me.

Fifty to seventy-five other people and I were sitting in Huxley meeting hall, spending six or more hours a day dancing, drumming, and singing. And then dancing, drumming, and singing every night. It was such a celebration!

Between these workshops, in the fall and winter I'd practice by myself. I would set goals for myself to learn certain rhythms before I saw Baba again.

After two years of attending his workshops, I asked Baba to be his student. He said yes. We both took this task seriously. I began to sit in the front of the class on his right side. He watched everything I did with an eagle eye. Even though it made me extraordinarily self-conscious, I asked for it.

It is painful to learn the drums so publicly. But what choice did I have? Baba was not going to give me a private lesson—he was a group teacher. I had one week with him, or maybe two, in the summer and one in the spring: just me and Baba…and sixty other people. I was driven to get the most out of my time with him. I went to learn EVERYTHING I was capable of learning. I had a young son I was raising and couldn't travel with Baba, which is what I really wanted to do—just to be with him and learn and learn until I got good enough—maybe even to play with the Drums of Passion band!

Baba taught me enough to have a beginning repertoire, and then he watched to see what I would do. It took me time to master simple skills, but I was passionate about learning. I was so sold on the power and energy of Baba's music, the force of his soul coming through his hands and his voice, the way he inspired people. *That's what I want to do*, I thought.

My Audition

After my third year of drumming, Baba would instruct me to play certain challenging parts. One was the top part to *Fanga*. This part is very simple, but it has a certain groove that you have to FEEL in order to play it well. The pull of the bottom accompaniment influences the top part, makes it funky.

So here I am, in the middle of class, given my big chance to show my teacher! I play through the phrase a couple of times before the pull between the bottom and the top begins to unravel my rhythm. Baba says "Stop," and tells me to go back to playing the bottom rhythm. That's the end of my audition for that five-day workshop.

Next workshop, six months later, he again tells me to play the top part. Again he stops me when I can't find the groove. So twice a year, I got to show whether I had learned anything since the last workshop. Never mind being overly excited or nervous! One shot, my dear. Better get it right.

Ouch—Teaching and Struggling

I began to teach classes in my third year. I taught what I really knew—Baba's rhythmic patterns, easy rhythms that I'll introduce you to in this book. It took me two more years to realize what was holding me back. I could play but I couldn't relax. Understanding the timing of the intervals between drumbeats sometimes eluded me.

Each year, twice a year, I took my private lessons with Baba (in front of the entire workshop of students at Esalen). In the middle of playing a rhythm, Baba would tell me, "Solo!" And I would take off—trying to create a tasty musical phrase that would stand out against the predominant rhythm. I staggered around a bit. Sometimes I felt at a loss, trying to understand how two rhythmic structures intersected. I stressed, trying to feel the tempo and at the same time hold onto what I was playing.

Worst of all was my intense self-consciousness. I realized that I could not hide my lack of understanding of rhythmic time. Everyone saw everything!

TaKeTiNa—Stepping into Rhythm

I decided to take a workshop called *TaKeTiNa*. My drummer friends said "It's all about understanding rhythm and time." Just what I needed! In the workshop, my first experience with *TaKeTiNa*, we stood in a circle, stepping patterns with our feet and clapping rhythms with our hands. Some of these rhythms coincided; some were independent of each other—a polyrhythm or cross rhythm. It was so easy. There was nothing to remember, no mistakes to be made. It was all flow.

We were encouraged repeatedly to allow ourselves to fall out of rhythm, and that falling-out was *an essential part of learning.*

What? I did not have to get it right? That's counter-intuitive to the way I was taught!

I felt such relief while stepping, clapping, and sinking into rhythm. It was enough to make me want to pursue learning *TaKeTiNa*. What I wanted was rhythmic competence: not to be afraid when playing with others, to rediscover the joy of playing!

This desire to understand rhythmic timing took me on a ten-year journey of study with Reinhard and Cornelia Flatischler. I learned to lead *TaKeTiNa* workshops and, in the role of rhythmic guide, to witness profound transformations in participants who engaged in workshops of rhythmic immersion.

Although I was most interested in healing my *own* rhythmic disability, I also learned more about leadership and how to create and lead a rhythm circle, and I ended up working for the Flatischlers. I organized their basic three-year courses as well as two advanced courses during the twelve years I worked for them. And in my time as their student I continued to explore the fabric and the underlying vocabulary of rhythm. I learned what makes rhythm such a profoundly healing path, an engaging inner process, and for me a deeply spiritual process.

What amazing teaching! *TaKeTiNa* teaches you to drop into rhythm with no instrument other than your body. It's hard for people to understand this practice who have not yet experienced the deliciousness of being held in the heart of rhythm.

Putting it all together

After fourteen years with Baba, and some time during the twelve years I spent with the Flatischlers, I began to synthesize what I had learned from these great teachers.

I learned as much of Baba's classroom repertoire as I could—dances, songs and drums—to the best of my ability. Baba gave me the building blocks, not only how to play the drum, but also to treat it as a medium, to create music, passion, ritual, and meaningful communal experience. He inspired a drumming culture that gives opportunity for anyone, anywhere, to learn how to drum and enter into the music. He used his knowledge of the importance of storytelling to give meaning to drumming—connecting what we play to age-old cultures. We can also learn to use the drum to call the sacred out of us, the magic. When I was with Baba, I just loved him and everything that came through him.

What Baba taught me is that you can call in the spirit realm through the instruments of voice and drum. You can set souls free.

He taught me not only about the power of teaching but also *how* to teach. How to contain energy—to put a lid on it, begin to cook it, and keep building the heat, keep building until everything takes off on its own. How to notice people and how to sense the group: see the group as well as hear it. How to intervene at the right moment with a story, or a side experience, or a body exercise—anything that can allow rhythm to be felt more directly!

Eventually Baba said "Solo!" again—and I did. I soared around the room and came back for a landing. It was sweet, not pyrotechnical. I spoke in phrases that corresponded to the drum patterns as well as the spaces between notes. My body listened and responded with its own creativity to the music. And—Baba smiled.

I knew that there must be others who had a hard time sensing and feeling how to groove— the magic of being transported by rhythm without thinking about it. I wanted to help them learn what I had learned, but faster and less painfully. I hope this book will help *you* find the groove.

An Interview with Baba Olatunji

From *Village Heartbeat*, Vol. 11, No. 2, March 1994

During a break in one of Baba's annual workshops at Esalen Institute, the extraordinary retreat center on the cliffs overlooking the ocean in Big Sur, I walked Baba to his room. When he opened the door, hot air blossomed out—it was hot inside, about as tropical as you could get. "Aahh, Africa," Baba exclaimed.

Olatunji is a man who has never needed to find his roots. He lives them each day; but he has chosen to do so here, in an America that often seems devoid of culture, family, community, and respect for its elders. How did he get here?

VHB: *I heard that you had studied at NYU to get a graduate degree in Diplomacy and International Politics. What made you go into professional music?*

Baba Olatunji: You mean getting paid for what I do?

I started as a student at Morehouse College in Atlanta. I was involved in drumming, singing, chanting, telling stories about the wonderful heritage of Africa and how it permeated world culture. I had no intention of becoming a professional musician, but circumstances led to it—the unbelievable questions students were asking when I arrived at Morehouse College in 1950.

Students would ask: "Is it true that Africans have tails? Do you live in trees? What do you really eat? Is it true that lions run through the streets in Nigeria's capital, Lagos?"

I didn't know what to do. I was surprised how little they knew about Africa. Where did they get their information? All they talked about were the animals, Tarzan and Jane. The image made you as an African feel you didn't want to be an African. It had a tremendous psychological effect on those of us who came here.

I came to the US with my cousin Dr. Akiwowo. We were both Rotary scholars.

I called my benefactor and asked, "What in the world is going on here?" He said, "Look, don't let anybody change your plan of what you came here for. You came to whet your appetite for knowledge and your locomotion toward your goal. You will face many obstacles. Keep your eye on the prize. Time will take care of the situation."

To maintain my sanity, I decided to talk about Africa, sing about Africa. I had been doing that for my own enjoyment when we came here by boat. I brought a little drum and I was singing to two American children who happened to be born in Africa as the children of missionaries. They were going to visit their grandparents in Texas.

That's how it all started.

So, instead of exchanging blows or fighting members of the student body, I started talking about Africa, singing folk songs, talking about how great the culture is.

I'd look at some of them and say, "You look like somebody from my village."

They'd say, "Oh no, I am not an African. I am a Negro." That's how it was.

I gave my first performance organizing a group, using students from the Atlanta University System. Those in colleges didn't want to participate or have anything to do with it.

I gave my first African show in 1953 on the Clark College campus, which was opposite mine because my college didn't have space for a show, didn't have a theater or an auditorium. We used a barn.

When I graduated from Morehouse, I came to New York instead of going to Boston University or the University of California, where I had a scholarship. I decided to come to New York because I saw so many people in Harlem who looked like people from my village. I promised myself that after the graduation I'm coming to New York. I believe that New York is a place that if I make it, it will be known all over the world, and I was right. So I went to NYU Graduate School of Public Administration and International Relations from 1954 to 1959, and I was put in the Ph.D. program. I completed all my course requirements.

I selected a subject matter for my dissertation that dealt with information that you couldn't find in any previously written material. The subject was "Critical Analysis of the Impact of Colonial Administration on the Communal Ownership of Land and how that has Affected Capital Development and Capital Formation in Nigeria from 1900 to 1950." NYU agreed to publish it if I could write it.

The thesis took in a period of five decades: how people left their farms to come to the cities believing their good is only in the city. People stopped farming. That was the beginning of colonial rule in the territories in Africa.

That was one reason, but also that was the time of social change in this country—in the Civil Rights movement. I was right in the thick and thin of it. In 1953 I was elected president of the student body. In 1953-54 was when the NAACP leadership changed, and they were appealing to the youth to become members. I was flown from Atlanta to New York, to the old Hilton Hotel, facing Madison Square Garden, where they had (gathered) 5000 youths. And I was brought there to talk to them, to give them inspiration that here's a foreigner from Africa elected as president of the student body. They never had a program like that before.

When I got back to campus in Atlanta, I went to speak before the student body. I got the student council to vote unanimously to make every student become a member of the NAACP for 50 cents.

Roy Wilkins was president of the NAACP then, and he appointed a young graduate from Howard University, Herbert Wright, to be the director of the Youth program. From there on, with the civil rights movement, with Dr. Martin Luther King, I was called to perform at fund-raising events all over: New York, Philadelphia, Boston, Washington, Chicago, Indiana. In fact I went with my drums to campaign for the first black mayor ever elected in this country, Mayor Hatcher in Indianapolis.

I was doing all of that, but had no money to go home and write my dissertation. So I couldn't go anywhere now. And nobody would give me a grant. Nobody was giving any African any grant at all. See, that's how my dissertation never got written.

I was contributing to the United Nations work with the children, UNICEF. The first recording that UNICEF put out, I have a song there, a lullabye about children. I attended a party at the end of 1954. The director of the UN choir was asking everybody from foreign countries to do something, a song from their homeland in their own language, and I did a chant to the god of thunder. He asked me "where did I study voice?" I said, "I never went to school to study voice. I sang in the choir at home and in the village." He said, "I'd like to introduce you to a friend of mine at Radio City Music Hall." His name was Ray Wright, the arranger of the symphony orchestra. That's how I was featured with a 66-piece Radio City Orchestra doing what was called African Drum Fantasy, which opened September 1958 for seven weeks at Radio City Music Hall.

That was my biggest break. The performance, with reviews in all five New York newspapers including the *New York Times*, led me to the *Tonight Show, the Ed Sullivan Show, To Tell the Truth*, and all the shows that were on television, and finally led to the contract to record *Drums of Passion* in 1959. So, that's how I became a professional. It was not planned, it was not designed. It was through a force of circumstance. In brief, those were some of the circumstances that led to it. Because when I found out how they were talking about Africa, the vision was so damaged that I had to take some kind of action. In order to maintain my sanity, I took the cultural route, that there is a cultural basis for our unity.

VHB: *So you began to teach as far back as then?*
Baba Olatunji: Yes. In 1950, from the very day I set foot on campus, I began teaching about Africa.

VHB: *And have you been teaching continuously?*
Baba Olatunji: I never stop. Not a year did I go away to do another thing. I've been persistent. Most people are doing it now because it is the thing to do, joining the bandwagon. I saw it. It was like seeing a vision. Even some of my countrymen from the early sixties said "Why perpetuate what Hollywood has used to insult Africa? Why play those jungle drums?"

That's what they called it. "Stop doing this," they said. I didn't give up.

VHB: *That leads me to my next question. When your recording of Drums of Passion came out, it was the first time for most of us that we had heard ANYTHING of African music or African culture or chanting. What have been some of the obstacles in bringing drumming to this culture?*
Baba Olatunji: You have to go back in history. Drums have been relegated to the background in this culture.

The people, the slaves, who first got here brought drums. When the people came back from the cotton fields, in order to really revitalize themselves and their energies and keep their spirits high they got together to chant and play drums. People would come from all over, a mile, two miles, three miles and come to celebrate and dance and then go back to get ready for the next day to work in the cotton fields.

They took the drum away from them.

Then they discovered that about twenty people were from the same family. They sent them to different places and divided the family. They broke the family pattern. They sent the man to one place, the other part of the family to Massachusetts. They just scattered them around to make sure that they were not together for the continuation and preservation of the culture and the language. They sent them to different parts of the states: the South, the Midwest and the North. So the drums were banned.

Now fortunately, Latin America and its music came along and did a little bit of preserving African culture in Latin America, in the Caribbean, and South America in general. I would say thanks to the Creator in general for that kind of influence of Latin American music, and its roots in African music. That helped to maintain a little bit of African culture in this part of the world. It was not really made known to the public what kind of music it is. In all recordings, drums were relegated to the background. They were not prominent in recording as they are today.

Nothing significant is said by the record companies. They didn't think much about it. They seldom featured percussion, the way it is featured today. So, for years, whatever you hear in any recording is played down. It is not promoted as a major part of a musical rendition, or composition, or performance. Those are obstacles even today, too. What we hear on radio and television is not really what we should be hearing. We are not hearing a lot of African music or recordings on commercial radio.

There is still a problem there. Sporadically, you hear a few stations playing my music certain times of the year, maybe once or twice in a month, whereas producers, programmers, make sure that certain recordings get played over and over again. So this way they are not really educating the public, they don't intend to educate the public about the significance of music. When *Drums of Passion* came out it was quite a revelation.

The young man who was responsible for signing me to Columbia was very aggressive, sensitive and inquisitive. He said, "Gee, I never heard this drum sound before. Go for it." After a year he was relieved of his duties as an A&R for Columbia Records. But he went on to become one of the great rock and rhythm & blues producers. His name was Al Ham—not black—but a Caucasian from Connecticut. But he was inquisitive, you see. So that was the luck in the recording of *Drums of Passion*.

But even then, we were trying to put it on an educational level—that to go with this recording there are dances, stories to go with it, so I asked them to let me go into the schools.

They said, "Oh no! You can't take this kind of music to the schools! Look at the name of your group! NO! We don't want to be using those kind of words in the schools."

Can you imagine? And what they say today on television, compared to then!

But in 1959 I succeeded in taking drumming and the stories about African drumming, chanting, and dance to New York schools, to New Jersey. Mickey Hart was a student who participated in one of my assembly programs.

VHB: *You were at my school on Long Island in 1959, too! Given that most of us taking workshops haven't been exposed to the sounds of African or Caribbean music, what advice can you give the beginning drummer?*

Baba Olatunji: Very important. Ask: "Why am I playing this instrument?"

I like it, I love it, I just want to find out about it, etc.

What do I want to do with it, get out of it? Ask your teacher this: "What can I do with the drum, what can I use it for? How can it benefit me?" Otherwise it can become a fad.

Then you can guide yourself, come up with a program leading to mastery of technique. So the drum will not be a thing that just becomes a room decoration. The beginner should be inquisitive enough to read about the drum.

There is no reason why anyone should believe that they can't aspire to be a master drummer. That takes a lifetime. You should never stop discovering something about the drum, except when you are playing. Then you play.

It's something if you play every day. You learn how to handle it, listen to it, play better, use it to express yourself more eloquently. It takes time.

The beginning drummer should not have the attitude that many people have of the drum: that it is an instrument that you can jump on and just learn to play in two months, three months, six months, a year. No. It needs to be respected, to be handled with the understanding it's going to take time before I learn this instrument. Many beginners confronted with this urgency want to know how to play it now. I appreciate their feeling and their excitement about it. But you don't feel the same way about the saxophone, trumpet, guitar. SO many things you have to put together to play it well. And it takes time. So, patience. Patience with yourself, because it's the discipline, to be a successful, efficient great drummer you need to discipline yourself and spend time upon time playing, trying to measure your own development—and most important, not to feel that you are in competition with anyone. "Oh well, we started studying together. Now he can do a better slap than I can." No, everyone has their own tempo, their own style. Some can get it fast. But remember: slow and steady wins the race. So, patience.

VHB: *Can you say something about the healing power of the drum?*

Baba Olatunji: Drums have evocative power. Someone might say: "Prove it to me!" You must experience it individually to really believe it.

There are little things you might notice. In a group, you might start playing, and someone you would never expect will get up all of a sudden and dance. There's a healing process going on.

In my discovery, there is a trinity involved. That's why I recommend students have at least one drum where the body of it is natural wood, not synthetic. The wood has a spirit in it. The skin has a spirit in it. And there is the spirit of the drummer.

A plastic head is okay for practicing, but you should have skin for playing. The spirit of the skin, the drum, plus the person playing becomes an irresistible force against any immovable object. That's number one.

Number two, every cell in your body and mind is in constant rhythm, what one of my students calls constant frequency. Everything we do is in rhythm. And I notice, whenever I get out of rhythm, that's when I always get in trouble.

VHB: *That's when we get sick.*
Baba Olatunji: It's natural. I notice that I can be somewhere at a dance where music can be playing. If it's good music, all of a sudden, some sound comes along. I jump up and say, "oh darling, let's dance!" What is the spark? How did it come about? What touches me? These are the things that you have to discover yourself.

When you know how to play, you will feel this inside. When you are playing inside the rhythmic patterns, you will feel it within yourself. You will feel elevated to a very high level. You become intoxicated. Not with liquor, but with feeling. Sometimes you have to stop and bring yourself down. It has happened to me. If you feel that way, imagine how the people who hear you play feel. You are playing for yourself as well as for them. So the healing process begins there.

We are still working on what it is, how does it happen. We may never come to know the complete answer, but we know that we can feel it. If the results are so profound, what the heck do I want to find out why for? In the words of one of my teachers: "There are many questions that may never be answered, and might be useless if known."

VHB: *You've seen—because of your work and inspiration—the growth of fledgling drumming communities. Do you have advice for them?*
Baba Olatunji: There is a school of thought in the United States that you can just put people together and they jam. And they feel good. What happens after that?

Well, they say, they organize themselves and get together. How long will that last? Is this going to be a fad? So we really have to put this on an educational level, that's why we need programs to make people more interested, not just that one community gathering with 400 people playing and they all beat together. They buy drums, they put them in their house, they still don't know anything about drums. You have to be very careful.

If it's just for a drum company to sell their product, we are telling them you have to contribute, so you have educational programs to follow it. You have drum communities that presenters come and say, "Okay. *Gun go do* is played like this: *Gun go do go do Gun.*" Give them three rhythmic patterns. Everybody can play that, of course. People are not stupid. But when they finish, what happens to that? They buy drums, you leave them, they're left hanging.

You provide leadership to them, an opportunity for them to be studying about drums, to be reading about it. That must be looked into.

When drumming communities have their first gathering, they should ask their presenters, "What are we doing next? Are you going to come back six months from now and do the same thing? What should we be doing, practicing?"

When we talk about people who can play piano in this country, there's millions. We want to be able to say the same about drummers, that there are millions who can play the instrument very well. Not just for us to get them together to have a jam session, so we can sell some drums.

VHB: *Laughs*

Baba Olatunji: We want to sell drums too, but hey, come up with an educational program, an idea for having a center in the community, where people can come from other places to teach, and people in the community will come to it. If they can't afford to come to Esalen they can bring somebody in who will teach.

People doing community workshops, drum circles, leave people hanging. We all can do that, those who know how to get an audience going. We can do that. Give them one or two beats, teach them a song and they feel good right then. Is that the end of it? Ask: "How do we continue?"

This is not a criticism, it is an observation. I'm hoping by the 21st century five if not seven of ten will have drums in their homes to bring together friends and family to chant, meditate, play and energize themselves.

VHB: *Thank you, Baba.*

 CHAPTER ONE

Getting Started

The Principles of Drumming

Drumming is about sound. And it is also about silence. Babatunde Olatunji, the great Nigerian drummer and my inspiration and teacher, used to say that the drum has three main uses: communication, social interchange, and healing. In my experience it is also a *practice* and a *path of presence*. By practicing the drum, we open ourselves to a new way to focus and open to the present moment.

The drum is an instrument for communication

In the rural areas of Africa, a slit drum or log drum would be used to send messages. Its tonal sound can be heard from far away as signal or code—the bush telegraph.

I once heard the master drum "speaking" the eulogy at a funeral in Ghana. I was told that the drum recited proverbs, symbolic of the person who had passed on. One message had a bit of double entendre; "*this man was known to sow many fields*" could mean more than one thing!

The drum can speak and communicate. I'm not always sure of what it's saying, but you can tell when someone is speaking. And you can definitely tell when they're screaming!

The drum is a means of social interchange

There are many kinds of labor that require repetitive movement. In Ghana, when you pound the cassava root with a mortar and pestle, you establish a rhythm: A-B-A-B. Speaking "A" is the motion of pounding the root with the stick and "B" is when liquid is added to the cassava and it is kneaded into a glutinous mass called fufu.

When people hoe the earth, plant the seeds, and harvest, they use the rhythm of chants and songs to make the work easier. When fisherfolk cast their nets, they too can accompany their work with rhythm. Since the beginnings of warfare, drums have also accompanied soldiers into battle, creating cadence to override fear.

The drum can inspire all these endeavors along with the voices. Synchronized actions accompanied by rhythmic sound allows for ease and fluidity of movement!

And in the human life cycle—birth, death, marriage—the drum and other rhythmic instruments are a critical part of creating the sacred in rituals and ceremonies. Music becomes a part of the community's social structure: village MTV.

The drum is a healing tool

Something magical happens when you sing and drum simultaneously. Sometimes it seems as though the mind is used to operating on only one channel at a time. I can play the drum, yes. I can sing, yes, But together? The mind can no longer hold its attention on only one event. When I force my attention to open to a broader spectrum, an amazing thing happens. I'm in an awake, altered state. I'm not spaced out; I have more free attention, relaxation, and heightened awareness.

You can sing a chant that comes from another culture or make up your own. Become your own sound healer.

The drum is a path of presence

The more you can stay in the field of free attention, the more easily you can call on this expanded state of awareness. Healing, creativity, insight, and inspiration all come from expanding and stretching into your potential for presence. Drumming is a great way to do it.

A drummer who uses the modality of rhythm to become more *present* can use the drum as a way to enter into magic—a special, unplanned for, and totally hoped-for paradise called *groove*.

Become aware of your sense of control in *how* you play—with rhythm. Awareness of the space *in between* the notes you play becomes as important as your notes. It's also important to be attentive to how you are sitting or standing. There is a physical rush in playing the drum with good body posture.

When you add another person to the mix, listening becomes crucial. It is the difference between chaos and music. Listening, connecting and relaxing while playing opens the door to more communicative drumming. Then there are three playing: two bodies that can be counted and one more entity called rhythm.

Rhythm is its own being and it guides us. And there is another benefit. When you begin to visit rhythm more and more often with others, you become a softer person, less competitive. You feel confident in your ability to be a human being with other human beings in play, and you can let go into a bigger force. You can't control it but you can invite it, by practicing, listening, and feeling as you play.

Why Drum?

There are many reasons to drum. One is instant gratification. Connect to the drum skin with your hand or a stick and sound emerges. Get two or more people together to play and you have energy and sound. You get and give attention. There is the potential for connection and creativity.

Get two or more people together who have learned to play rhythms from specific drumming cultures, and you introduce the music and art of that culture to the world.

The other day I was marveling at this path called drumming. I reflected on how many people I have met from different persuasions, cultures, and lifestyles, because of our mutual love of drumming and rhythm. Here are some things that make drumming and rhythm so compelling.

Cooperative Community

Although drumming is happy as a solitary event that can occur at the beach, in the woods, or in your living room, drumming is exciting (and of course amplified!) when playing with others.

Drumming can be improvisational. This is what happens in a community drum circle.

Drumming also can take the form of orchestrated playing: a planned set of orchestrated rhythms of a particular ethnic style or self-created music.

Whenever we play together we have the possibility of something synergistic happening, something magical, unpredictable. Drum music creates the most amazing groove—everyone is so locked in that we are like one giant animal, lumbering though the undergrowth, or…a positive train wreck!

Because we are so new at nonverbal, cooperative play (well, maybe since kindergarten) it is an experiment in truth. My friend, Arthur Hull, a master drum circle facilitator, reminds us to a) listen, b) know when to add something, and c) know when to get out of the way!

But if at first you don't succeed, try. Then try again.

Passionate Playing

In the hope of a wild groove occurring, we can take another approach. Take turns playing different accompaniments or little rhythmic statements. Learn to listen to how these parts sound in tandem with one another. If there are a few strong drummers who can really hang out in a primary groove, they will juice up the rhythm machine for others to have the room to experiment.

The main thing is to learn to support each other, and more importantly, support the music!

Play a simple bottom groove often to refresh your palate. Enjoy the people you play with and what they add to the circle. You don't have to like the person you are drumming with in order to create music together.

How to Choose Your Drum

Here are some things to consider when you're buying your first djembe drum. There are similarities to buying your first car. First, what's more important to you, aesthetics or efficiency? A gorgeous car in bad mechanical shape is no bargain. If you see a drum that is so, so beautiful, filled with gorgeous carvings, but it sounds like crap, it's a crapshoot as to whether or not a new head, rings, and rope will improve the quality of its sound. And in drumming, sound is more important than visual aesthetics.

For All Drums

Whether you are purchasing a djembe, conga or synthetic drum, look at the overall appearance of the drum. Does it sit on the ground levelly? Is its head on straight? Does the drum need a stand to be played? How heavy is it?

A manufactured drum like a Remo or LP is made from fiberglass or some other epoxied-wood product. It can still be an effective tool, especially if you're playing at the beach, in parades, or anywhere out in the elements. Synthetic skins are an acquired taste, but Remo Belli has been changing the Remo heads over the years and the latest versions sound better and last longer.

TEST DRIVE! Listen, listen, with your ears, with your heart. Don't just get wowed by its looks. Listen to the speaking voice or *go-do* first, versus slap or bass (see Drum Language and Basic Techniques, page 7). That speaking voice is the most important sound on the drum.

Find out where the drums you are interested in come from. Many *djembes* are being made in Ghana. Find out if there is a Fair Trade policy. It's good drum karma!

For Djembe Drums

1. **Shell**

   If the shell is wood, check for cracks, holes, and critters living inside. Look for defects in the body. If it's hand carved, is the inside of the shell roughly cut? Is the bearing edge (top lip) of the drum rounded?

2. **Drum Hardware**

   Take a closer look at the rings that hold the skin on the drum and the rope or hardware that pulls the top ring to the bottom ring. Is the head evenly placed on the drum body? The rings should be close to the head of the

Here are examples of good shells with nice proportions.

drum. Check out the rope. Make sure it is not too stretchy and has no major nicks or tears in it. How close are the vertical ropes and are they evenly spaced?

3. Head

Are there skin blemishes or small tears? Has the head been shaved? Is there a gamey smell? Synthetic skins are great for variable weather conditions. Some folks are sensitive to the degree that they don't want an animal skin on their drum. In that case a synthetic skin is a great alternative.

4. Weight

How heavy is your drum? How much can you, or do you want to, haul around with you? You can get a case with wheels, but you will still have to load and unload it from your vehicle.

And finally....Do you love it? Absolutely love it, the sound, the look, the feel, the height—everything?

Drum Care

Your drum is an instrument. The drum becomes a *voice* for you to express yourself. Baba used to say: "The head of the drum is the skin from the animal world; the shell of the drum is tree wood from the vegetable world; and combined with *your* spirit they make an irresistible force for good and for healing."

Of course there are synthetic drums, such as the ones from Remo mentioned previously, and we can imagine that this same blessing extends to them.

There are basic ways to care for your drum. Here are some.

DON'T LEAVE YOUR DRUM IN THE CAR!

This exposes your drum to extremes of heat and cold. The wood of the shell of the drum can take only so much expansion and contraction without stretching the skin, which will affect the sound. You would not leave your dog, cat or child in the car, so why leave your drum? Yes, it is an inanimate object, but it is also an important tool, and a relationship that you are developing with yourself.

- Keep your drum in a case when you travel with it.

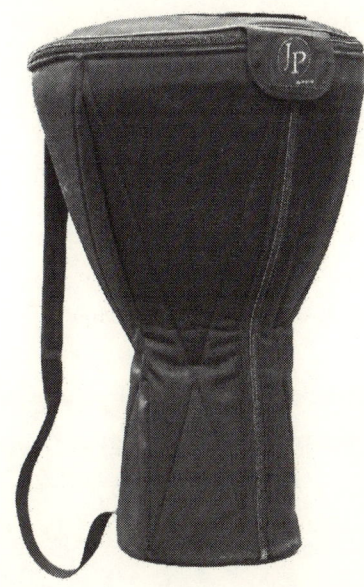

If you can't buy some kind of spiffy bag with fur lining (I'm kidding, but who knows?), at least get yourself a sturdy duffel bag and towel for the head of the drum with an all-purpose bungee cord to keep the towel in place. If you are traveling by plane make sure you have lots of protection for the head of the drum. You can make a thin plywood circle to cover the top of the drum and secure it with a padded drum hat to prevent any kind of damage. Paste FRAGILE stickers all over your case!

- Take the drum out of the case when you get home. It's easy to forget to play your drum when it's in a case!

- Don't use your drum as a table. It is not a fancy drink stand or a place to write notes or rest your legs. How would you like it if someone put their legs on your head?

- It is not necessary to use any extra oils for the head of the drum. The oil from your skin should be enough for the head of the drum. You might use kerete or shea butter on your own hands, which will, over time, soak into the drum skin.

- Have the head of your drum replaced by a reputable drum builder or "wrangler" every year or so. Changing the head changes the sound of your drum—Tune it up! If you are careful with your drum, you probably could wait longer than a year, but over time the quality of your sound will change. I highly recommend Drumskull Drums in Santa Cruz, CA. They really have the science of changing the head, looking for any cracks that might have appeared on the shell of the drum, and getting the rings to fit right around the head of the drum and below the bowl.

- Humid climates require different drum care. Keep a terry cloth towel wrapped around the head of your drum when you are not playing it. Goatskin drums will get soggier in humid climates over time.

- Don't forget the power of ritual. The drum can be a conduit to trance and altered states of real growth and development with ceremony. I like to feed my drum. I give it thanks and gratitude. Sometime I symbolize that by making a small plate of food and a drink to place near it. My drum likes gin—Bombay gin.

I know it's my drum's choice because I can't stand the stuff and it's expensive. So, when I celebrate something and my drum is nearby, my drum gets to celebrate too. Drums like candles, incense, and all the things that give us a sense of nuance. It doesn't have to make sense. Just do it. You create the sense of a deeper connection to your drum by acknowledging it as an important tool on your road to self-discovery…even if it seems foolish.

Drum Language and Basic Techniques

Drum Alphabet

Every drum culture has a drum language, or a way to mimic how the drum speaks. Baba created his method, which many Westerners use: *Gun* (pronounced goon) indicates the bass note, *go* and *do* (doh) the tones or speaking voice, and *pa* or *ta* the slaps. On a *djembe* or *ashiko,* imagine James Earl Jones with his rich bass voice (*Gun*), Johnny Mathis with his smooth middle sound (*go* and *do*) and Pee Wee Herman with his high squeak (*pa ta*). This is the cast of characters for our basic sound alphabet. I say *basic* because as one studies different styles of drumming, there are other sounds that may be added: muffled slaps, closed slaps, flams, rolls, heels, tips, and others. But for now it's sufficient to deal with these three sounds.

If you've committed yourself to learning to drum, you'll need to build basic technique and stamina, of course; but you'll also need to start living in rhythm—what I call building the rhythmic hard drive—and something more mysterious than that: becoming aware of the spaces between beats—the intervals—as well as the actual beat itself.

Technique

Learn how to make a bass (*Gun*), tone (*go do*), and slap (*pa ta*) consistently! Below are illustrations of the positions for *Gun* and *go do*.

In the video **www.WholePersonDrummingBook.com (Basic Technique)** you can see the body movements required for making clear sounds with a drum. These techniques may differ from the way you were taught originally or the way your current teacher is guiding you. Try them out and see how they help and/or hinder your playing. This is the **basic** repertoire of sounds for most of the rhythmic patterns you will learn to play here.

Remember that the drum, although predominantly seen as a rhythmic instrument, is also a melodic instrument. Lessons in technique can be a little frustrating, but necessary. You are learning to build muscle memory and hand placement memory, and to build a container that allows you to play rhythmic songs competently, clearly,

Gun | Go Do | Pa Ta

and for extended periods of time. Also, technique helps you to stay focused. When you focus on what you are playing, you enter directly into the present moment.

There is nothing like kicking out the jams with some really good musicians and walking away with your hands glowing, but no injuries.

Playing with Flow

The moment that tension comes into your body, the drum responds. You can actually *hear* the stress in playing; there's less differentiation in your bass, tone, and slap. Another clue is loss of dynamic—meaning that everything sounds loud, loud, loud!

You don't want to tighten up as you play. Even if you're excited, playing can remain fluid and easy. One way to stay cool is to practice with FLOW.

Each note as you play sets up the technique for the next sound. Imagine that your hands are bouncing on some huge trampoline! No stress, just flying!

Start with *Gun:*

To produce the *Gun* sound, your hands are more or less horizontal to the head of the drum, and one hand moves up and over, describing a smooth half circle from the edge to near the center, making contact—*Gun!*—then bouncing back.[1]

For *go* or *do*, you bring your hand back along that half circle toward yourself to contact the drum a little closer in. As you bounce off the *go* or *do*, lift the hand straight up as if you're waving at someone. From this position, your hand falls toward the head of the drum, heel of the hand leading. This is preparation for the slap.

As you make the slap (or *pa ta*) your hand lifts off the drum (the follow-through for *pa*), with the fingers more vertical than the *go*. Then slowly and gradually, turn the hand again along the half circle to come down toward the center of the drum for *Gun*.

In the beginning, exaggerate the flow and the shapes you are making with your three notes.

Notice that your hands are always in fluid motion, not staccato.

In time, the shape of the half circle and the vertical hand preparation for the *pa* or *ta* will become a natural way of playing the drum. Your hands will look like, and more importantly, feel like…*flow*.

You will see as you play at higher tempos that flow is an important way for you to be in the groove with the least amount of stress in the body.

This is not to say that you won't be breathing harder, or working the rhythm, but you will be able to drum effortlessly and freely, with ergonomic, easy movements.

Unit Box Notation

When I first started drumming, I wrote pages and pages of notes with *Gun go do* written in accents and closer together and farther apart to denote space. Even though I had learned how to read music a long time ago, writing rhythms was challenging. I didn't want to translate rhythms into the Western method of writing music. For me, it took the mystery out of *feeling* the rhythms.

Baba would write his rhythmic syllables and songs on the board and we would all copy everything down assiduously. But really, unless you had an inner recording that kicked in when you read these syllables, it was just a bunch of weird words on a page. So, instead of reading or writing, I *taped* everything. I still have boxes and boxes of Baba cassette tapes from the fourteen years of classes, along with copious notes.

Finally, I learned how to use *unit box notation* to write down and practice Baba's (and other teachers') rhythms. Unit box notation is a system for writing out rhythms, similar to traditional musical notation. It is particularly useful to show the different parts that add up to a complex rhythmic texture. It is also important to see the spaces or intervals between the notes/events.

In Western musical notation, sounds and units of time are expressed in *notes* and *bars* or *measures*. The time signature of a piece is the number of beats per measure, expressed as a fraction, such as 4/4. The number on the top tells us how many beats (pulses) are to be contained in each bar or measure and the number on the bottom tells which kind of note is used to describe the beat: quarter, eighth, sixteenth, etc.

So in the time signature 4/4, the notation indicates that **there are four beats in each measure,** and **the quarter note signifies one beat.** It does *not* mean that each measure has only four quarter notes. It means each measure has only four *beats*. **In this case a beat is a unit of time, not necessarily of pitch.** These beats may contain half notes, quarter notes, eighth notes, rests, whatever the composer wants, but all note and rest values must combine to equal no more or less than the top number (or numerator) of the time signature.

Tempo indicates the number of pulses per minute. It is probably an attempt by the brain to impose what is heard within bodily rhythms (heart-rate, breathing, walking, and chewing) into an external time structure.

For complex drum rhythms, unit box notation makes it easier to show the entire rhythmic pattern. It's still within a repeating time cycle, like a measure, and it can still be expressed as a time signature, like 4/4, but *the "unit"—the rhythm, the pattern—is bigger than one measure.* The multiple lines of boxes can show multiple drums as well as all the other instruments that contribute to the rhythm, including hands, feet, claps, bells, and voice.

I will use unit box notation throughout this book. All charts are available for printout at www.WholePersonDrummingBook.com (Unit Box Notation Handout).

Here is a chart—a notation—showing your first, simple rhythm to a count of four (Simple Rhythm to a Count of Four chart, pictured on page 11, for a person who is right-handed). The count is at the top, then right and left hands on the drum, then the drum syllables.

Let's look at the same structure of four beats with intervals *(*Four Beats With Intervals chart on page 11*).*

These are just a few examples of how to show rhythmic patterns.

Watch the Free Instruction Video: Unit Box Notation, at **www.WholePersonDrummingBook.com.** It may help you find your own way into reading and writing notation.

Remember to move your hands sequentially as you overlay the rhythmic pattern with your voice.

Simple Rhythm to a Count of Four

Time	1	2	3	4	1	2	3	4	1	2	3	4
Hand	R	L	R	L	R	L	R	L	R	L	R	L
Drum	*Gun*	*Gun*	*go*	*do*	*Gun*	*Gun*	*go*	*do*	*Gun*	*Gun*	*go*	*do*

Four Beats With Intervals

Time	1	2	3	4	1	2	3	4	1	2	3	4
Hand	R	L	R	L	R	L	R	L	R	L	R	L
Drum	*Gun*		*go*		*Gun*	*Gun*	*go*		*Gun*	*Gun*	*go*	*do*

Rhythm Syllables

Here is another way to look at musical *events* (notes) and *intervals* (space). Imagine that the notes are the tip of the iceberg and the space is what's below the surface. It is silent but not empty. There is life in the absence of sound. Once you figure out where the spaces (or *intervals*) are, you can speak the intervals while you play the notes. Spoken syllables can help you understand this essential relationship between sound and space.

I use two ways of notating time: counting 1-2-3-4 as noted above, or using *TaKeTiNa* rhythm-syllables or "vocables," that is, Ta-Ke-Ti-Na. I prefer using the *TaKeTiNa* syllables[2], as they allow you to identify a construct of 1-4 without thinking. *Ta* is always one, *Ke* always two, and so forth. For example (see Rhythm Syllables Chart, page 12):

You can also use other *TaKeTiNa* rhythm syllables for different subdivisions. For subdivisions of two, we can use *Ta Ki*. *Ta* is 1 and *Ki* is 2.

Rhythm Syllables								
Vocables	Ta	Ke	Ti	Na	Ta	Ke	Ti	Na
Time	1	2	3	4	1	2	3	4
Drum	Gun			Gun	Gun		go	

Similarly, we use *Ga Ma La* vocables for subdivisions of 3; *Ga* is 1, *Ma* is 2 and *La* is 3.

I prefer using vocables, as they allow you to identify a construct of 1-2, 1-2-3, or 1-2-3-4 without thinking. This way you can learn to use imagery (rather than numbers and counting) and develop an intuitive sense of rhythm.

Isolating the space apart from the note rather than simply playing the rhythm can be initially frustrating. You have to slow the rhythm down to see/feel these elements. As you "grok" space, you can understand how intervals influence the context of the rhythmic phrase you are playing. Understanding space is the key to arriving at *groove*, the ineffable, exciting voltage between events and intervals—sound and silence!

Footnotes

1   See Free Instruction Videos at www.WholePersonDrummingBook.com (Rhythm Notation)

2   The TaKeTiNa Rhythm Process, developed by Austrian percussionist Reinhard Flatischler, is a musical, meditative group process for people who want to develop their awareness of rhythm. *The Forgotten Power of Rhythm: Taketina*, by Reinhard Flatischler

Chapter Two

Learning the Basics

Drumming Warm-Ups

Here I am, at age sixty-seven. I have never stopped drumming since I began at forty-one. But I will never be like my friend Alalade's kid, who drums at a cruising speed of ninety miles per hour. I wish I could. I am envious, and maybe if I went to the gym and worked out every single day…no, I tried that.

And still. Where I couldn't develop super speed, I worked on technique: clear sounds of bass, tone, and slap, and how to consistently make the same note occur. In the ten years I studied with Reinhard Flatischler, founder of *TaKeTiNa*, I grounded myself in rhythmic understanding. I am still envious of pyrotechnical drumming displays, but not doing badly for entering elderhood.

So this brings me to how I teach drumming now: I do warm-up exercises. I have gleaned them from dance classes, yoga classes, chi gung, and my good friend, Sanga of the Valley. There are older women and men in my classes, and I want them to take care of their bodies in the same way that I am learning to take care of mine.

Here are a few exercises that are really helpful to use *each and every time* **before** you drum.

Sitting Posture Exercises

Sit up straight. Find a way to lower your shoulders and allow your shoulder blades to slide down your back. Imagine that you have giant angel wings on your shoulder blades and the weight of them pulls your shoulders down and

Air Drum | *Shoulder Circles* | *Zombie*

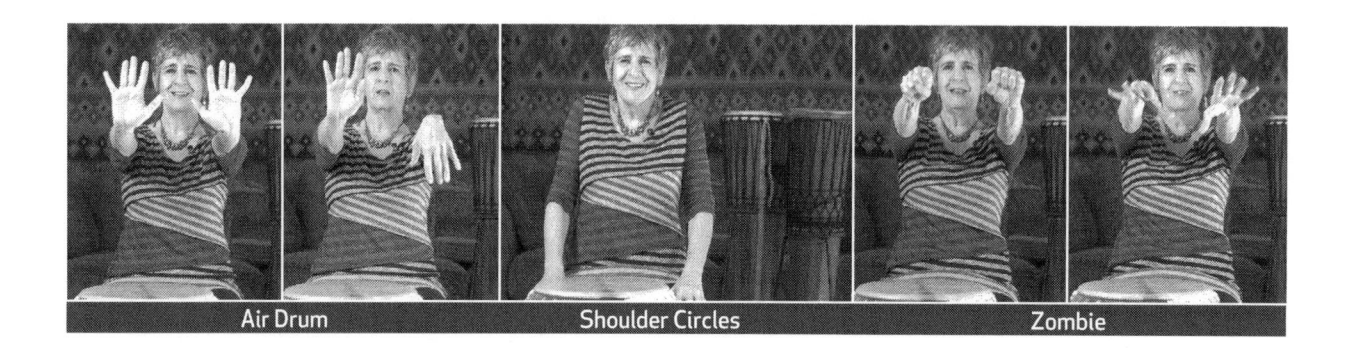

opens up your chest. Tuck your chin in slightly so you have a long neck. Breathe. Nothing should feel forced or strained. Also, if you like, you could imagine a giant kangaroo tail coming out of the bottom of your spine that you can lean back into. (I got the kangaroo tail from Cornelia Flatischler.)

Joint Exercises

See video: www.WholePersonDrummingBook.com (Drumming Warm-ups).

1. Put your hands straight out in front of you at shoulder level with locked elbows. Just use the wrist and hands, not the arms! Air drum. Start slowly.
2. Circles with the wrists. Hula dancing hand circles with straight arms, locked elbows, again at shoulder height. Pinkies lead as palms face away from you. Do it again with the palms facing toward you. (I hate this one!)
3. Shoulder circles. First, circle back. Go for ease of movement. When you circle forward it should resemble the butterfly stroke.
4. Elbow circles. Turn your hands facing away from you and place them on your shoulders, right hand to right shoulder, left hand to left. Bring your elbows together. Make elbow circles going around clockwise. Reverse and make counter-clockwise circles.
5. Stretch your arms out in front of you with your elbows locked and your arms at shoulder level (like a zombie). Make your hands into fists and wrap your thumbs around the fists. Open your fingers straight, with energy, and then make the fists again. Imagine that you are sending bolts of light or love out the tips of your fingers! You will feel heat in your forearms.

Overhead Stretch

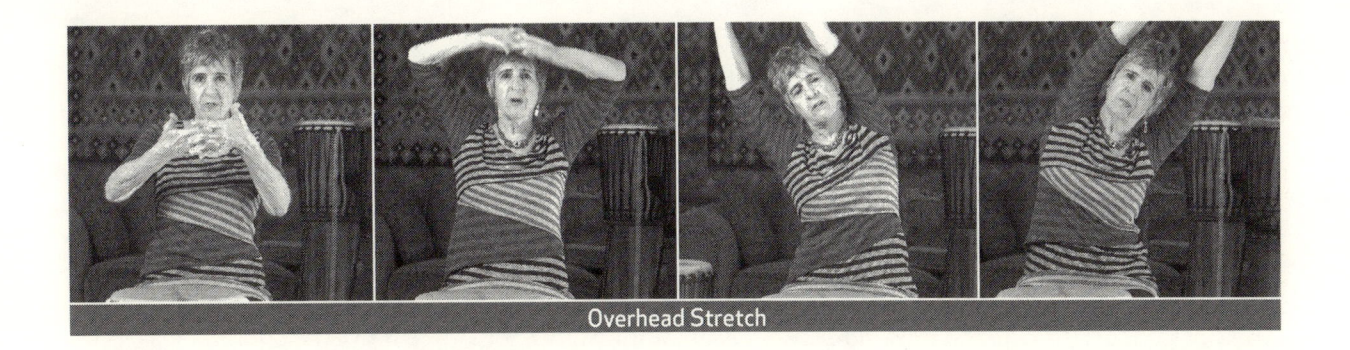

Flexibility and Stretching

1. Right index finger over your head and into your left ear. (Sounds weird, but it works.) Pull gradually across the top of your head to stretch out your neck muscles. Let your left arm hang down to create a counterweight. Reverse to the other side.

2. Lace your fingers together in your lap. Turn your hands inside out and stretch them above your head with arms straight. See if you can move them slightly behind your head. Undo the stretch. Re-lace the fingers with your other hand in the top position. Stretch. Undo. Let your arms hang at your sides for a moment.

Breathing

Become aware of your breath. Notice the inhalation and exhalation and the pause before the cycle of breath begins again.

Begin to drum at a very slow pace. Breathe rhythmically with your drumming. Breathe in for four counts, out for two, and pause for two. Or find your own way to rhythmically connect to your breath WHILE drumming.

Finally, sit up straight or stand straight while you play. This is an energetic art—one that requires your focus. As you pay attention when you play, your body will recognize more ergonomic ways to move. Drumming will energize and strengthen you.

And…smile on the inside while you play!

Rhythmic Structures

Through the investigation of rhythm that I learned from *TaKeTiNa* and the rich cultural material that I learned from Baba and other teachers, I began to see how *rhythmic structures* or groupings of rhythmic patterns inform movement on the drum and in the body. Think of creating a building out of blocks. You have to have a ground floor. In rhythm, you can think of the pulse as the musical and rhythmic foundation.

That basic pulse is a rhythmic *event* that occurs more or less consistently, like our own heartbeat. Another kind of information is found *between* each of the pulses. We call that the *sub-division pulsation*. Any space can subdivide into equal portions. For the rhythms in this book, the subdivisions will be in two, three, and four.

Rhythms in Four/Four

When you subdivide a rhythm into four pieces, like the one below, all of the beats within a four-beat subdivision are equal, and yet they each have their own individual influence. They could be likened to the framing between the beams in a building—how the weight is distributed evenly between one beam and another.

I have shown this chart of four beats in numbers and also using *TaKeTiNa* vocal syllables.

Four Beats: Numbers & Vocables					
Vocables	*Ta*	*Ke*	*Ti*	*Na*	*Ta*
Time	1	2	3	4	1

Beats will have a different feeling when combined into small groups called *motifs*, which are two notes that are side by side, such as *Na Ta* or *Ti Na*. Each carries a particular feeling or groove in the music. When you understand these groupings of rhythms, or the different positions of pulsation within four beats, you're starting to understand the different colors or feels within a *rhythmic structure*.

Queen's classic song, "We Will Rock You!" has one kind of rhythm. Hear it in your mind's ear. WE will WE will ROCK you. **ONE** two **THREE** four **ONE** two **THREE** four **ONE** two.

"We Will Rock You!"															
Ta	Ke	Ti	Na	Ta	Ke	Ti	Na	Ta	Ke	Ti	Na	Ta	Ke	Ti	Na
1	2	3	4	1	2	3	4	1	2	3	4	1	2	3	4
We		will		We		will		rock	you						

2nd and 4th Beat								
Vocables	Ta	Ke	Ti	Na	Ta	Ke	Ti	Na
Time	1	2	3	4	1	2	3	4
Clap		X		X		X		X

Beat one gets the emphasis. But Reggae, Ska, and Soul music live more in the second and fourth beats of 4/4. If you watched the audience at the start of a performance by Bob Marley, who is the most highly recognized musician in the world of reggae, you'd see about a quarter of the people clapping on *one*. (Throughout this book I will italicize the *one* because it is our marker for the initial pulse.) But friends don't let friends clap on one and three (it's a joke, mon). Before long, everybody's closer to the groove.

Polyrhythms/Cross Rhythms

Polyrhythms, sometimes called cross rhythms, involve two or more separate families of beats, each with its own interval and feeling. *When these are played at the same tempo, these two worlds can come together and become a third "song," a third creative being.*

It is a challenge to feel all of these rhythms at once, through direct experience. We cannot do that without deeply understanding the nature of these pulsations. It takes time, trust, and immersion to enter the feeling of rhythms and hear the group groove. Don't worry, we'll practice more polyrhythms later in Section 4, Rhythms that Rock!

Polyrhythm of Four and Three												
Vocables	Ta	Ke	Ti	Na	Ta	Ke	Ti	Na	Ta	Ke	Ti	Na
4 Subdivision	1	2	3	4	1	2	3	4	1	2	3	4
Vocables	Ga	Ma	La	Ga	Ma	La	Ga	Ma	La	Ga	Ma	La
3 Subdivision	1	2	3	1	2	3	1	2	3	1	2	3
Group Song	go			gu	ba		gu		ba	gu		

3 and 4 together = go, 3 pulse= gu, 4 pulse = ba

When you understand the structure of the rhythm, you can begin to appreciate the feel, the groove of music, and you can also understand how to re-create it, how to appreciate it in *drum orchestration*, where one part of a rhythm creates tension with or against another. That makes us want to move, groove, dance!

Learning Rhythms

There are lots of ways to learn about rhythm: by movement, by becoming curious about intervals, by breaking down rhythmic elements and their relationships to each other and becoming familiar with them. However, rhythm *lives* through direct experience or presence. We cannot *think* rhythm. Thought is slower than the moment of a note or an interval on the drum. We have to be in the moment.

I will say this about learning rhythms. We learn in different ways. (See more about Learning Styles, page 25.)

The first, more conscious way involves analysis, reading, hearing, practicing:

- The analytic mind remembers patterns.
- The eyes read unit box notation or notes.
- The auditory memory remembers rhythm tunes.
- Muscle memory finds the most economical way to play the rhythmic pattern or remembers the sequence of hand positions.

The second way we learn is much more difficult to notice or prove. It happens in our sleep. It is the assimilation of the rhythm into our body awareness as a *felt* pattern. The rhythm becomes a part of us, like learning to speak in another language.

As we study forms that are more rhythmically complex, we must give our body/mind the space to hear, feel, and sense the new landscape of sound. We can walk to it, eat to it, dance to it, and find every way possible for the rhythmic figure or pattern to become a part of ourselves. And that also takes time.

There is no race to learn rhythms. At a certain point I stopped going to class. It wasn't because of lack of new patterns to learn. Rather, I had to digest and understand all the previous rhythmic patterns I was introduced to. So take your time!

Learning the Flow in Four

Each set of rhythms has a different character and moves the body in a different way. Our general default position is always to start any rhythm with our dominant hand.

In this set of rhythms I invite you to try working with your non-dominant hand. How does the non-dominant hand affect the articulation of your sounds and feeling of competency (or klutziness)?

First, begin to play combining sounds—in other words, lead with the sounds *Gun Gun*, moving your hands forward into the middle of the drum, and *go do* moving back toward the edges. Check in with your technique (page 27).

				Flow in Four				
Vocables	*Ta*	*Ke*	*Ti*	*Na*	*Ta*	*Ke*	*Ti*	*Na*
Time	1	2	3	4	1	2	3	4
Drum	*Gun*	*Gun*	*go*	*do*	*Gun*	*Gun*	*go*	*do*

Begin with the rhythmic voice accompanying your strokes on the drum: speak *Gun Gun go do Gun Gun go do.* Stay with your voice and the accompanying movements of your hands on the drum. At some point, after becoming comfortable speaking these syllables while playing, switch to speaking the numbers *one, two, three, and four.* You may notice that the mind has a harder time tracking when you are saying numbers. (I notice a mental dryness when speaking numbers.) Reminder: If you are starting with your dominant hand, you will be playing the one and three with that hand.

Make a map in your mind of these hand positions and their names/numbers.

Now you have brought to your awareness two voices that are allies. One defines what your hands are doing while you are drumming, and the second indicates that each of these elements has a different placement in the four-beat subdivision of time.

The third shift is to change the voice to the syllables *Ta Ke Ti Na*. Now each syllable not only is a number but has a name in the family of four. Find this lesson at **www.WholePersonDrummingBook.com (Flow in Four)**.

Calling the Elements

First, stay in the flow of *Gun Gun go do* and switch your voice to the *TaKeTiNa* syllables. Then try the variations below.

Flow in 4 - Variations								
Vocables	Ta	Ke	Ti	Na	Ta	Ke	Ti	Na
Time	1	2	3	4	1	2	3	4
Drum	Gun	Gun	go	do	Gun	Gun	go	do
Song 1	Ta				Ta			
Song 2			Ti				Ti	
Song 3		Ke				Ke		
Song 4				Na				Na

1. Sing all four syllables over the course of eight beats—two complete cycles of four beats—in a tune of your own making. Experiment to make the tune pleasing to yourself. Enjoy how your voice and hands are combining to weave the fabric of this rhythmic structure.

2. Single out the syllable *Ti*. Call it out and notice it in your dominant hand as the drum note *go*. See what happens when you make *Ti* the center of your awareness. Feel what it's like to speak a syllable that's not the *one*! If you lose your place (or to refresh yourself) go back to singing all four syllables to mark your way back to the present moment.

3. Next select *Ke*. The trickiness of *Ke* is that you are playing on your non-dominant side, close to the *one*. See if you can clearly call the *Ke*. Start to make a song beginning on the *Ke*. If starting on the *Ke* is difficult, speak ugh for the *one* and then start your song: *ugh Ke Ti Na or ugh hey bum ba*

4. Finally, find the *Na* with your voice. This is the most fun element to find! Right before the *one*, it has a snap to it. Again the note is on the non-dominant hand. Give yourself time to locate it in your voice and visually with your hand.
   Some more variations to play with are in the chart below.

5. Sing *Ta* and *Ti* (or 1 and 3). *Ta* and *Ti* are on the dominant hand. It will be easy to identify the connection between your voice and your movements on your dominant side. Feel the stability of the composition. Sing an independent song. Ex: Hey-go-Hey-go-

Flow in Four - More Variations								
Vocables	Ta	Ke	Ti	Na	Ta	Ke	Ti	Na
Time	1	2	3	4	1	2	3	4
Drum	Gun	Gun	go	do	Gun	Gun	go	do
Song 5	Hey		go		Hey		go	
Song 6	Hey	go	space	go	Hey	go	space	go
Song 7		go	space	go	space	go	space	go

6. Sing *Ke* and *Na* (song 2 variation). This is really a great way to see the pulling power of the *one*. When you begin to sing, you might notice if your focus is on the dominant side, meaning that you are still aware of the *one*. If you have not continued to be aware of the *one*, you may notice that your mind has reoriented you toward thinking that the 2 and 4 became the 1 and 3.

7. Sing without the *Ta*—Notice on the chart that the offbeats we are singing on the 2 and 4 are now without any reference to the *one*. You can give yourself support by noting the first *Gun*. Right after that *Gun*, speak "*go (space) go*." Again notice that these two notes are located on your non-dominant hand. Don't be surprised if these offbeats are hard to find.

Here's how you can do this same exercise with **stepping and playing** the drum—first on the *Ta* and *Ti* for balance.

Have your drum on a stand or simply use a bungee cord to anchor it to a chair. Stand behind it and begin by stepping in place, like taking a walk. Now verbalize the four rhythm syllables or numbers, speaking the *Ta* (or 1) when landing on the right foot and *Ti* (or 3) when landing on the left foot. Then begin to gradually add your hands, playing the same pattern as before: *Gun Gun go do*. Sense the space between your footsteps. Notice how it feels to play and step simultaneously!

Play and Step Simultaneously								
Vocables	*Ta*	*Ke*	*Ti*	*Na*	*Ta*	*Ke*	*Ti*	*Na*
Time	1	2	3	4	1	2	3	4
Drum	*Gun*	*Gun*	*go*	*do*	*Gun*	*Gun*	*go*	*do*
Step	R		L		R		L	

Finding the 4/4 Groove in the Body

In this chapter we experience a 4/4 bell pattern with our bodies, using clapping, stepping, and speaking. The bell pattern is also called *clave*, or the framework of a particular rhythmic structure. **Clave** is a Spanish word meaning "code" or "key," as in key to a mystery or puzzle (see also The Bell Rules, page 63). Here are two simple exercises to help you find this bell pattern (this particular 4/4 clave—there are many!) with your steps and claps.

Exercise 1
Introducing Training Wheels and Offbeats

Again step with the right and left feet, like taking a walk. Now verbalize the four rhythm syllables or numbers, speaking the *Ta* (or 1) when landing on the right foot and *Ti* (or 3) when landing on the left foot. This is a grounded way to feel the four beats in the body. I call this step pattern in 4/4 Training Wheels. Now speak the *Ke* (2) and *Na* (4)—the offbeats—*between* the footsteps. Clap on the *Ke* and *Na*, while stepping on the *Ta* and *Ti*. The verbal pattern for this is: step clap step clap. Pay attention to the second clap—the clap on the *Na* (the offbeat), represented by a bold **X** and underlined X. It will be important in our second exercise: **Training Wheels**—basic exercise to find the 4/4 beat.

Exercise 1: Introducing Training Wheels & Offbeats								
Vocables	*Ta*	*Ke*	*Ti*	*Na*	*Ta*	*Ke*	*Ti*	*Na*
Time	1	2	3	4	1	2	3	4
Step	S		S		S		S	
Clap		X		**X**		X		**X**

Exercise 2
Working with a 4/4 Clave

Begin the Training Wheels step pattern again. This time our first clap is on the *one*, the *Ta*, where the right foot lands and our pattern begins. Notice that there are eight more steps and/or sixteen beats before we return to the place where this first clap and step starts. We call the amount of space from the first note to the end of the rhythmic phrase a *cycle* of sixteen beats.

Bring into your voice the first *Na* (or 4) after the *one*. It is found after the second step and before the third step. This is the only clap that is not on a step, but between them! It's this clap that makes the clave special.

Exercise 2: Working with a 4/4 Clave																
Vocables	*Ta*	*Ke*	*Ti*	*Na*	*Ta*	*Ke*	*Ti*	*Na*	*Ta*	*Ke*	*Ti*	*Na*	*Ta*	*Ke*	*Ti*	*Na*
Time	1	2	3	4	1	2	3	4	1	2	3	4	1	2	3	4
Step	R		L			R		L		R		L		R		L
Clap	X			**X**			X				X		X			

Hint: You can say: Step-(space)-Step-Clap to practice finding the *Na*.

It's always good practice to make up a phrase like this one to create a map of information regarding the steps and claps. It can help you to feel grounded in the rhythmic pattern in the body without thinking or analyzing. Find this lesson at www.WholePersonDrummingBook.com **(Free Instruction Videos: Adding the 4/4 Clave).**

Add your third clap by finding the *Ti* on step 4. Make sure that you add each clap gradually and in your own timing. Clap 4 is also on a *Ti*.

Another clue: both *Ti's* can be found on the *left* foot.

Finally we add the final clap on the last *Ta*. Take your time finding each clap! When you complete this pattern with your body, stay with it for a while. Sing it, groove with it. When you are ready, pick up a bell and play it!

Exercise 3
Stepping On the *One*!

This second version of the exercise takes a little more time to learn. It is the same clapping pattern, but this time the feet are only stepping on the *one* of the pulse.

The second clap right before the step creates tension between the foot and clap (hand). Intuiting or feeling the two *Ti's* will be easier because we experienced the rhythm in the body in the previous exercise with *Ti* in the footsteps. You can see how building trust in one's ability to find rhythm directly in the body allows us to gain confidence in learning rhythm without an instrument. Eventually, the body understands where the offbeat resides, even if the mind doesn't. Also, the tempo will get faster in this (non-training wheel) version. This change allows us to use a more natural walking step pattern on only the *one*.

Enjoy!

Exercise 3: Stepping On the *One*!															
Vocables	Ta	Ke	Ti	Na	Ta	Ke	Ti	Na	Ta	Ke	Ti	Na	Ta	Ke	Ti	Na
Time	1	2	3	4	1	2	3	4	1	2	3	4	1	2	3	4
Step	R				L				R				L			
Clap	X		X				X				X		X			

Learning Styles

After my son was born, a friend gave me a series of books: *Your One-Year-Old, Your Two-Year-Old*, etc., by the Gesell Institute and Louise Bates Ames. The books described what skills a child of that age would typically develop. In many cases my boy's development didn't match the patterns in the books, and it took me a while to realize that there was nothing wrong with his development. He was mastering different skills than the ones in the book. I couldn't place him in the book's development spectrum, because his growth was unique to him.

It's the same for learning to drum and learning within rhythm. Each of us comes with a different set of potential skills and develops them in a different way. Some people are kinesthetic/tactile learners—they seem to effortlessly understand how to imprint muscle memory and connect it to the notes they play. They understand how to integrate technique into playing almost immediately.

Some people are auditory learners. They learn by hearing the patterns and reproducing them from the sound. They might not learn as effortlessly as a kinesthetic, but they can remember rhythmic patterns more easily than others.

Some people are visual learners. They have to see what others are doing to learn. And that sometime presents additional problems. What they see across from them is a reverse image of what they need to do, and requires them not only to translate what they see, but to transpose the reverse image as well. That makes it a challenge for them to learn and stay in rhythm.

If I see a student intently watching me from across the circle, I suspect they are visual learners and will invite them to watch the students on either side of them instead. I encourage non-visual learners to do that as well; it helps them begin to see their fellow students as helpmates. It becomes easier to build a community if we learn to rely on each other.

In drumming you learn that even if you don't *like* the person sitting next to you, you can learn to *love* them. When you fall out of the rhythm and they are still holding onto the pattern, you find your way back with their help. On the next rhythm you might be the strong one helping them return. Drumming together builds a community through mutual support.

When I first began drumming, I had trouble letting go into rhythm. I had played guitar for many years, but timing and rhythm on the drum was far more difficult than playing chords and strumming. Every time I played—in a drum class, or with other drummers, or even on my own—all I heard were my mistakes. And I did not accept mistakes as part of the process of learning. I was very critical of myself every time I fell out of rhythm. **That's why I teach people that we must each learn in our own timing, in our own way.**

Whatever your default primary learning style, start where you are. Learn the skills needed to stay in rhythm, to vary dynamics (soft or loud) and build a rhythmic memory with songs you can access whenever you want to.

Leave the critic outside the door of the classroom.

To be skilled at drumming you must learn a new way of seeing, hearing, and interacting with the world around you, new ways of moving your body to make sounds, and new ways of relating to the people who drum with you. That can be hard, but it is even harder when you react to being a beginner. That's when you tangle with the superego or the critic.

When I see someone grimacing in class, I know that they are not reacting to me or the other people in the room. They're listening to their internal critic, who belittles them every time they mess up.

When you're learning to drum, you're sitting in a safe place with a community of people having the same experience. You're not juggling hand grenades, flying a plane, or doing brain surgery. No one is going to die when you miss a beat. You are here to learn. Why make it harder by hitting yourself over the head?

Knowing that each of us comes to the table with a different set of strengths should be enough to know that if you don't understand what you're playing today, you might tomorrow. In fact, there is a very good chance that if you do what you can—keep it simple or play Root Rhythms (page 57)—you will get patterns much faster than if you shut down and don't listen to what is happening around you.

Yes, it can be an ego-killer to be slower in learning, but it's not useful to expect more. You are learning technique, muscle memory, phrasing, timing, rhythms, and rhythmic orchestration and memory retention *all at once*. That can be challenging.

It is more helpful to have patience and humor and take a little bit at a time than to listen to the voice of the critic. The critic shows up as annoyed or irritated feelings that sometimes fly under the radar. The critic urges us to try *too* hard.

I say all this because I was and am a slow learner. I can play rhythms, but I do not play them well until I understand them, and that takes time. That is probably the main impetus to my becoming a drum teacher. No one was teaching beginners, and no one was teaching *how to learn* as a beginner.

Learning rhythms on the drum is learning a language. Along with this new language, there are new skills that are cross-referenced: body movement, body placement, muscle memory.

When you're learning a foreign language, it's best to immerse yourself—to be surrounded by people who don't speak your language. At some point, you begin dreaming and thinking in the other language; then you know you're starting to get it.

As I have said and will continue to say, falling out of rhythm, losing it, is *necessary* to deeply connect to rhythm. For drumming to begin to move us, we've got to have the balance between attention or focus and relaxation. Like the old saying: "Sometimes I play the drum and sometimes the drum plays me," peak moments do happen when the drum plays you! But until lift-off we learn to practice our art and craft and enjoy the fruits of learning together.

How to Practice with the Drum

One of the things I love about drumming is the practice of it. Whether you play often or not, working on technique rather than just banging away is essential in my book. And it reaps great rewards!

There are other reasons why practice is advisable.

If you only take out your drum when a jam happens, there is a very good chance that A) you may injure yourself or B) you may poop out. Practicing consistently for shorter periods (with concentration) builds greater rhythmic attention. When you are a consistent, grounded center, it is easier playing with those who are beyond your skill level—and there will be times when you are the strong one for those "younger" in skill.

Practice Drum Technique

As explained in Drum Language (page 7), with each hand drum there are three basic sounds: bass, tone, and slap. To review, in Baba Olatunji's drum language we call them **Gun** (the bass note), **go do** (the tones or middle sounds), and **pa ta** (the slaps or high sounds). Depending on your "axe," there are different ways to learn to play these notes efficiently and ergonomically.

Sitting down to HONESTLY listen to yourself will help improve the consistency of your playing and make you a more confident drummer. Your drum can become a melodic instrument as well as a rhythmic one!

I am a big believer in the five-minute method. Attend and intend to play with concentration on your bass, tone, and slap, **three times a week for five minutes**. Really focus on each sound. Work on only one thing for each session; for example, Tuesday morning is working with the bass note, or *Gun*. Listen to how it sounds and feels to play with your **dominant** versus your **non-dominant** hand. If you spend less time with more concentration, you will probably want to play more because you LIKE how you sound!

Spend a good amount of time working with your **non-dominant** hand. Leading rhythms from your weaker side allows you to become stronger and quicker in developing your reflexes. The difference will be obvious in a short time.

Build Stamina

Building stamina to play for long periods of time is part of your training as a drummer. Have one of your five-minute sessions include stamina drills! Take a rhythm that is simple and continuous. Start out with short periods of single licks to a count of four, as shown in the box notation: *Gun Gun go do*. Begin to increase your speed. The moment that your sound gets muddy or unclear, slow it down again.

Exercise: Build Stamina											
1	2	3	4	1	2	3	4	1	2	3	4
R	L	R	L	R	L	R	L	R	L	R	L
Gun	Gun	go	do	Gun	Gun	go	do	Gun	Gun	go	do

Rather than going only for speed, drum slower with alternate sprints to get your breathing to become a flow instead of an in-and-out gasp. Do this as many times as you can and see if your speed with **clarity of sounds** doesn't improve. When you get to your top speed, hold it as long as you can! Breathe a lot. Stay with the rhythm until it drops away from you. And then do it over again.

Here is another exercise I use with all my students. By adding the *pa ta's* you now have a more complex rhythm to speed up! We have the combination of speed and technique to work with. Play at a slower tempo to ensure precision with sounds, *Gun Gun go do* and *pa ta*.

Exercise: Stamina, Speed & Technique							
Ta	Ke	Ti	Na	Ta	Ke	Ti	Na
1	2	3	4	1	2	3	4
Gun	Gun	go	do	Gun	Gun	pa	ta

Gently speed up until you lose the clarity of your notes. Stop. Start over. Repeat again.

Be honest about it. You will begin to actually play faster, and you will like how you sound! This is another great way to develop clarity and power and ease in your playing.

You will have harnessed an energy that can be quite compelling.

Build Your Rhythmic Hard Drive

Tape your classes. Listen to them. Develop associated imagery or songs with the rhythms that you hear. Walk to the rhythms, dance to the rhythms, eat to the rhythms.

Let them become a part of your inner landscape like rhythms that you listen to and like on the radio. See if your timing is right.

More Practice Tips

- Walk, jog, or swim—anything that is repetitive movement and gets you into a rhythmic flow rather than discrete activities.

- Leave the phone in the other room when you're practicing! The mind hates to focus on just one thing. But you KNOW you can make this time sacred for five minutes.

- Try to find a practice buddy. Even if you can't always play together, you could remind each other to give attention to your sounds. Also, if you have forgotten a rhythmic pattern, your practice buddy might remember.

- Finally, practice can be a meditation on sound. Sing with your drum. Baba always said that when you sing and play simultaneously, the drum becomes a tool for healing. This is true for me. When I sing and play, all the worries, all the world stuff that gets me, melts—and I am left with a feeling of calm and deep connection to myself.

I hope this information will serve you!

Drumming Classes vs. Solo Work

As you are about to begin your drum studies, here are a few points to be aware of.

When I bought my first drum, I was so excited, but it was a bit intimidating to start on my own. I didn't sound that great as a beginner playing by myself. My poor drum sat in the living room, lonely, for a few weeks while I got up the nerve to play. My drumming sounded so blah and uninspiring compared to the full sound that I heard in Baba's class, but Baba wouldn't be back for six months.

I found that drumming is usually taught in a class rather than one-on-one. There are definite positives to being in a group as you start to learn. You are carried by a wave bigger than yourself. You can hear the rhythms as they come from the group, not just yourself. Although I missed Baba, I found another class through Stanford University and entered a new world with a new teacher. So my advice is—Be kind to yourself as you begin your path. Look for a beginners' class. And if you don't like that class or teacher, look for another. Allow yourself to be inspired!

Benefits of learning in a group

- **Relying on those with more strength than yourself.** In a cooperative learning situation, you are allowed to lean on and learn from others. It is good for those who are stronger drummers in the moment to learn to be mentors and give a hand.

- **Be where you are. If you forget the rhythm, show it. There is nothing to hide.** We are all learning together, both individually and collectively. We have our individual path within the group. As the group itself learns, it morphs together into a united being called a community or a collective. It is amazing to see a group synch. The strengths and weaknesses all balance out to a yummy hum.

- **Joy of the group song.** The other day I was teaching a class in Raleigh, NC. I didn't know anyone in the class very well, and for sure they didn't know me. A majority of the class didn't even know each other. We learned the parts, split them up, started the engine. When the music hit it, it was amazing! We were no longer individuals, but a group with a common purpose. We were bound together by the music. It was beautiful, juicy, and groovy. There was a smile on everyone's face, a feeling of camaraderie. (Maybe members of Congress should learn to drum together before they try to get anything else done.)

- **The family that drums together hums together.** I am a child of my times. I gravitate to events and groups that engender peace, love and harmony. When I see it enacted in my drum class not once, but over and over again, it gives me great hope for the future. We don't have to love each other—we need to learn to coexist within a feeling of common purpose.

Challenges of learning in a group

Many of us have old wounds from our previous classroom experiences. The trauma of learning shows in various ways: cringing when the teacher scans the room, peer pressure, embarrassment about a wrong answer. If you have residual learning scars, you might be intimidated in your first drum classes.

You might hide behind other drummers and air drum. Or you might get swept away by the act of making sound without paying much attention to your body. In passionate playing, you can easily hurt your hands. That could be discouraging.

We are tender beings. We want to be liked. We want to be good at whatever we attempt to do. None of us wants to feel inadequate, especially publicly. Sometimes we develop different strategies in drum class to look more competent than we feel.

Here are a few examples of trying to hide while playing in a group:

- **Big motions or movement.** Too much tension can lead to spastic overplaying. If you were playing a *tabla*, *riq*, or *dumbec* (which are smaller hand drums), flailing or gross motor movements could destroy the instrument! On a *djembe* or conga, big movement also means big sound and the possibility for big bruises. Have you ever seen a really good drummer with tape all over their fingers from playing the drum? It's unlikely. Relaxation is the way to get those super-big motions to become more fluid. Smaller movements will still allow your drum to sound without flailing!

- **Very small motions or movement.** A good way to disguise what you don't know is to minimize your footprint in the class. Much easier on the hands, but just as hard on the spirit to put yourself in a little box! Breathe a little bit more and you will expand. Your drum voice will begin to resonate more. It is okay to take up space, to learn at your own pace.

- **Using your eyes instead of your ears to drum.** Visual learning in drumming usually takes us out of the moment. When we look rather than listen for our cues we have to take an extra step to translate the movement we see into rhythmic information to play. Try to develop your *rhythmic memory* by speaking the syllables that you are drumming rather than seeing them. You will find that you can play more easily by bypassing the visual.

- **Glazing over and spacing out.** Sometimes we need a break from the intensity of focus required to play. Spacing out allows that moment to disengage. The down side is that we could be spacing out while the rhythm or instructions begin! No worries. Take a breath and begin again.

Forgetting the rhythmic pattern, missing the entrance to the rhythmic pattern, playing at a different tempo—these will happen sporadically until you really understand and own a rhythm. All these so-called mistakes are natural and even necessary to the acolyte rhythmist. However, it is challenging to the ego. Arthur Hull, drum circle facilitator and trainer, coined the phrase: "drumming ego death."

One of the reasons I became impassioned about teaching beginners is because of my own story.

I was afraid of being a beginner. When I made mistakes and got caught at them, I felt bad about myself and imagined (or maybe it was true) that others were judging me. Was losing it really so bad? No, but it re-triggered old feelings of em-bare-ass-ment and low self-esteem. I tried to hide, which made everything worse. It was important for me not to be seen as incompetent, to be allowed to learn at my own pace. The more I drummed with others and was afraid, the more I hid, or feared judgment. Finally, in the right setting I began to see that I was learning—slowly but surely. What I really learned was not to be afraid of being a beginner.

The good side to playing alone or one on one

After you have a certain amount of information under your belt, it's easier to play by yourself. When you have rhythms to play, technique to practice, or healing chants to sing with your drum as accompaniment, it's great to spend time playing for yourself. Musicians sometimes call it "being in the woodshed." It's a good time to tune in to your own expression.

And also, when you want to work on your technique, you can take a private class to work on more ergonomic ways of playing and honing the precision of your strokes. A private class can really iron out some of the kinks or habits that could use undoing. One hour can seem like (and be worth) a couple of days of intense scrutiny. When you are ready, the teacher is there.

Chapter Three

Path and Practice
Beginning Practice, Beginning Rhythms

As a teacher in an arts festival, I taught a group of new drummers. This beginner class was an hour session wedged between other events. In that time, the students learned a quick sample of how to play, where the notes are, and how to sing with the drum. They got it! It's always wonderful to see people bitten by the drum and rhythm bug!

Perhaps this was their first time playing the drum. Maybe it was something they wanted to do their entire lives. Can you imagine their excitement, not only to play, but to actually hear the music they created? It is beautiful to witness this opening into joy and magic.

As a beginning drummer how can you serve your own learning? Here are some ways you can create your own map for learning.

1. Start with basic languages

First and always is the language of the body. Pay attention to how you sit. Use warm-up exercises to ground yourself (see Drumming Warm-Ups, page 13). Starting with awareness of your body will remind you to play with more awareness. Of course, as you warm up, check in with yourself. Are you here—or are you preoccupied? Are you feeling open or closed? Excited or guarded? As the guide for your own process there is nothing for you to do but notice how you are when you arrive. The music will do the rest! Hard to believe but true.

Practice the language of the drum. Start with one note. Practice playing *Gun* with the right hand and left hand. (Remember tips found in How to Practice with the Drum, page 27). Review the notes *go* and *do*, with both hands.

2. Create some small challenges

Hand games. As you are drumming the note *Gun* with your dominant hand, raise up your *other* hand and wave it around. You have created a small challenge for yourself. Although it is a trick, doing two things at the same time will loosen you up. You can either do it right away, or get lost in which hand does what, or do it intermittently. In any case, this little exercise allows you to get a snapshot of how you deal with a little added stress and an interruption in your playing. Do you laugh, or tense? Watch your own reactions. It will tell you a lot! Does the rhythm disintegrate? Do you speed up or slow down?

Voice games. When you can alternate playing the bass note *Gun* with right hand and left hand as well as *go* and *do*, play another game. Play a simple rhythmic phrase. Speak out loud while you continue to play. Say anything: nursery rhymes, the pledge of allegiance, anything! The brain may have a fart and hands may flounder for a bit. These interruptions are fine! Find your way back to the rhythm after a brief interruption. What happens in your body? Do you grimace? Bite your lip? Feel frustrated or confused? Laugh? Stay in the rhythm? There is no right answer, there is just information that you as the student want to observe. You begin to see when you lose the rhythm with these games or when you can remain in rhythm effortlessly. Losing the rhythm and finding it is important and necessary to the growth and evolution of your learning.

Notice when you're out of rhythm. How do you *know* when you're out of rhythm? What do you see or feel that might show it? It is much more difficult to learn when you don't know that you are out—out of tempo, out of rhythm, out of synch.

3. Notice how speaking the rhythm and playing the rhythm are the same

Speak random rhythms using *Gun's* and *go-do's* and then play them on the drum. This gives you the opportunity to play from the drum language instead of reading notes or imitating someone else. Speak each rhythm and then play. See examples 1-4 in the chart below.

Speaking and Playing the Rhythm							
Example 1	Gun	Gun	Gun	Gun	go	do	go
Example 2	Gun	Gun		Gun	Gun		go
Example 3	Gun				go	do	go
Example 4	go	do	go		Gun	Gun	Gun

If you have a difficult time with one of the patterns, repeat it several times. Again, notice how you learn. Do you get it right away? Do you struggle? How does your body feel? Are you spacing out? You don't have to draw conclusions or make judgments, just see the information.

And of course, you can make up your own!

> Each of us needs time to settle into ourselves.
>
> We all have our own timing to connect to rhythm.
>
> Each of us has the possibility of healing—
> by dissolving inherent judgments about our ability to learn.
>
> Each of us can heal our past wounds
> by being in rhythm in the present time.

4. Practice beginning rhythms

The rhythm Congolese 4/4 has its root syllables (see Root Rhythms, page 57). It is a wonderful beginning drumming rhythm. Any beginner can play! One of the great things about it is that the dominant hand *begins and ends* the rhythm figure.

Congolese 4/4 Rhythm								
Vocables	Ta	Ke	Ti	Na	Ta	Ke	Ti	Na
Time	1	2	3	4	1	2	3	4
Drum	Gun		go		Gun			
Step	R		L		R		L	

Another great beginning rhythm is Baya (see more in Baya and Intervals of Four, page 60). This rhythm starts with the first four spaces playing hand over hand: *go do go do*. It is followed by three *Gun*'s with space between one *Gun* and another.

We will return to these two rhythms later.

Baya															
Ta	Ke	Ti	Na	Ta	Ke	Ti	Na	Ta	Ke	Ti	Na	Ta	Ke	Ti	Na
1	2	3	4	1	2	3	4	1	2	3	4	1	2	3	4
go	do	go	do	Gun				Gun				Gun			

Singing and Playing the Drum

I have been blessed by teachers who taught—from the git-go—that you sing and play the drum simultaneously: Baba, Sanga of the Valley, Ma Boukaka, Samba Ngo, and others. This a MAJOR benefit for drummers, rhythmists, singers, and dancers. It is almost like we have more than one antenna, but most of us only use one channel at a time. When you sing and play at the same time, you can't hold on to a linear perspective. You let go. And gradually you can hear both channels at the same time. (I know this because I was the WORST drummer in the world when I began to learn drumming. I couldn't hold onto to what I was playing, let alone sing a song on top of it.) When you begin to open both channels your vision broadens and you are no longer as caught in the sole perspective of ego.

Developing this dual skill allows us to drop into an altered state of consciousness quickly, allows us to be more relaxed and less in control.

From the first day that we walked into class with Baba, we learned how to sing and play the drum simultaneously. The African arts pose this lovely challenge: sing and play the drum, or sing and dance.

I cannot think of a better way to get out of your head.

"Oh no," says the ego. "I can't do that!"

Actually you can, and if you want to get to a place where your drumming naturally flows and does not depend on your concentration, you will. Start with the obvious: sing a song on the beats/notes that you're playing.

Here is a rhythm called Conga (i.e. conga line) where you sing on every note that you play. Play and sing the top line three times (3X) before singing the end of the song (1X).

The more that you have the opportunity to sing ON the notes, the more confident you will feel when you can perceive the drum music going on in the background and your vocal song flying on top of the rhythm!

In the beginning it is important to sing <u>on</u> the notes even if you're just practicing *Gun go do*. Eventually, you can sing other syllables than the notes you're playing.

Try this song: *Abana ki-lem dy-o*. This is a Baba song about a sailor from West Africa.

Sing each syllable separately: ah-bah-na-kee-lem-die-oh.

The beginning of this song starts <u>before</u> the *one* (or the first beat.)

Conga																
Vocables	*Ta*	*Ke*	*Ti*	*Na*	*Ta*	*Ke*	*Ti*	*Na*	*Ta*	*Ke*	*Ti*	*Na*	*Ta*	*Ke*	*Ti*	*Na*
Time	1	2	3	4	2	2	3	4	3	2	3	4	4	2	3	4
3X	Gun				Gun				Gun			go				
	con			ga					con			ga				
1X	Gun		Gun		Gun		Gun		Gun			go				
	we		le		we		le		con			ga				

Try this song: *Abana ki-lem dy-o*. This is a Baba song about a sailor from West Africa.

Sing each syllable separately: ah-bah-na-kee-lem-die-oh.

The beginning of this song starts <u>before</u> the *one* (or the first beat.)

Abana															
Ta	*Ke*	*Ti*	*Na*	*Ta*	*Ke*	*Ti*	*Na*	*Ta*	*Ke*	*Ti*	*Na*	*Ta*	*Ke*	*Ti*	*Na*
1	2	3	4	1	2	3	4	1	2	3	4	1	2	3	4
															A
ba		na		ki	lem			dy			O				
Gun			go	do				Gun			go	do			

The "A" occurs on the four before the *one*. This is called a pick-up note. The next syllable, *ba*, lands on the *one*. After the start, the rhythm and song remain on the beat—easy to sing to.

For beginning students of all kinds, developing a sense of singing on the beat builds confidence—so you can eventually try singing away from the beat. This ability to sing and play simultaneously will develop on its own, but you have to practice opening to it. It's kind of like trying to find your balance in the tree pose in yoga, or learning to ride a bicycle. Eventually you cannot imagine that you ever had difficulty balancing!

Two Becomes Three (the Cross Pattern)

The cross pattern is one of the easiest rhythms to play. And it can also be one of the hardest!

The trick is whether your body will easily allow you to go into a pattern of switching the lead between your dominant and non-dominant hands. About eighty percent of my students get this change right away. There are always some (I was one) who overthink the whole thing and end up paralyzed and flailing.

There are lots of ways of teaching this pattern. Lately I prefer to go through the door of learning by allowing *two* to become *three*. You'll see what I mean!

Sit in front of your drum (or in front of a table if you don't have a drum) and begin by alternating your hands (dominant and non-dominant) in an evenly spaced pattern:

R L R L R L R L R L R L

Notice the feeling of two. One note is played with the right hand, one with the left. This is the world of two or duality. You can use Baba's drum alphabet and call the hands *go* and *do*, or a numeric notation 1 and 2. Later we will add the third *TaKeTiNa* notation.

Play in Two												
Vocables	*Ta*	*Ke*	*Ti*	*Na*	*Ta*	*Ke*	*Ti*	*Na*	*Ta*	*Ke*	*Ti*	*Na*
Hand	R	L	R	L	R	L	R	L	R	L	R	L
Time	1	2	1	2	1	2	1	2	1	2	1	2
Drum	*go*	*do*	*go*	*do*	*go*	*do*	*go*	*do*	*go*	*do*	*go*	*do*

Play in Two, Speak Three												
Vocables	Ta	Ke	Ti	Na	Ta	Ke	Ti	Na	Ta	Ke	Ti	Na
Hand	R	L	R	L	R	L	R	L	R	L	R	L
Time	1	2	1	2	1	2	1	2	1	2	1	2
Drum	go	do	go	do	go	do	go	do	go	do	go	do
Voice	Ga	Ma	La	Ga	Ma	La	Ga	Ma	La	Ga	Ma	La
Voice	1	2	3	1	2	3	1	2	3	1	2	3

While your hands continue playing in twos, let your voice speak in three.

In the beginning if it feels a little confusing, return to the original structure—speaking "one, two"—to stabilize yourself. Feel the hands tracking two, with the dominant hand always on the *one*.

Once you can easily overlay the three vocally, begin to notice that the *one* changes hands. First, it is your dominant hand that says *one*, then it is your non-dominant hand that is *one*.

Now, move the hand that is *one* toward the center of the drum for the bass note *Gun*, like this:

Start from Two - Play in Three/Cross Pattern												
Hand	R	L	R	L	R	L	R	L	R	L	R	L
Voice 1	1	2	1	2	1	2	1	2	1	2	1	2
Drum	go	do	go	do	go	do	go	do	go	do	go	do
Change	1	2	3	1	2	3	1	2	3	1	2	3
Voice 2	Ga	Ma	La	Ga	Ma	La	Ga	Ma	La	Ga	Ma	La
Drum	Gun	do	go	Gun	go	do	Gun	do	go	Gun	go	do

Left dominant

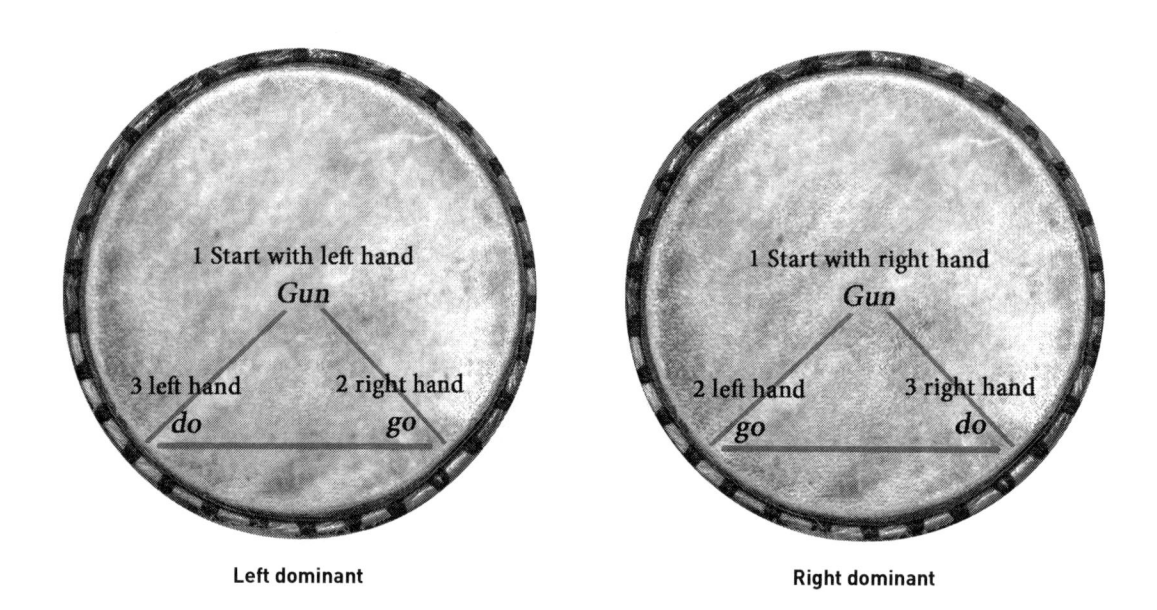

1 Start with left hand
Gun

3 left hand
do

2 right hand
go

Right dominant

1 Start with right hand
Gun

2 left hand
go

3 right hand
do

If you look down at your hands, they are now inscribing the pattern of a triangle.

As you begin to pick up speed with the pattern, you can notice the feeling of *flow* in your hands. Also notice if your state of consciousness has changed. Now the mind can relax and let rhythm guide you.

Another way of tricking yourself into alternating hands in this pattern is to slow down the movement.

Move the hands super slowly so you can track that the hands are always alternating. I do it by speaking "right, left, right" as one group of three, and then when switching lead hands I speak "left, right, left." By doing it slowly enough I can track my hands and make sure that I don't double hit with one hand.

If you get too frustrated by not being able to track the changes in class, there are two alternatives.

The simplest is to play only the *Gun's*.

This allows you to experience crossing from the right to the left hand without being flooded with too much information. It is a great choice (aside from the possibility of drumming ego death) because it allows you to hear the *one* (or the pulse) and also feel the crossover from the right to left hand. You can learn a lot by LISTENING to the notes that you are not yet able to play.

The second choice is to simply leave out the last two notes of the pattern. Then you can get the beginning of the phrase—alternating the hands and notes while feeling the "cross" of the *Gun* from the right to the left—with a SPACE that lets you gather yourself to begin again.

Simplify the Three												
Hand	R	L	R	L	R	L	R	L	R	L	R	L
Vocables	*Ga*	*Ma*	*La*	*Ga*	*Ma*	*La*	*Ga*	*Ma*	*La*	*Ga*	*Ma*	*La*
Time	1	2	3	1	2	3	1	2	3	1	2	3
Drum	*Gun*			*Gun*			*Gun*			*Gun*		

The cross pattern is a great foundation rhythm, one you can use for all your practice sessions. Play it often! You can use it to work on your technique—making sure that your right hand *Gun's* sound the same as your left hand. Then work on your right and left hand *go-do's*. As I mentioned before, you can also use this as a stamina drill to increase both your speed and duration of playing.

Another Choice in Three						
Hand	R	L	R	L	R	L
Vocables	*Ga*	*Ma*	*La*	*Ga*	*Ma*	*La*
Time	1	2	3	1	2	3
Drum	*Gun*	*do*	*go*	*Gun*		

Baba's Rhythmic Patterns

Baba started almost every workshop with this set of scales. Learning it was part of the repertoire of his music. I think it is a great exercise, because it takes you from simple to more complex forms. We play each of the six patterns four times. Once you learn the sequence, try going up and down the scales. Play 1 to 6, then reverse the order and play 5 to 1, and down the patterns from 2 to 6. Once you become proficient in the sequence, you can begin to play the patterns in your own order and create with it. Baba's rhythmic patterns are a good set of building blocks.

These scales are in a time signature called 6/8. As I explained before, Western musical notation uses notes, measure, and time signatures. 6/8 time means that in each measure (or musical space) there are six beats, and an eighth note is used for a single beat. Here is what it looks like in Western musical notation.

But that is for those of us reading music. In the teaching of African drumming music, we are relying more on hearing, feeling, and moving to the music!

Now for Baba's rhythmic patterns 1 through 6.

Notice the cross pattern (XP) at the bottom of the chart. The cross pattern is a timekeeper.

When you play Baba's rhythmic pattern *with* the cross pattern, you can hear the intervals, or the time in between the audible notes.

Baba's Rhythmic Patterns 1 Through 6												
Vocables	Ga	Ma	La	Ga	Ma	La	Ga	Ma	La	Ga	Ma	La
Time	1	2	3	1	2	3	1	2	3	1	2	3
Pattern 1	Gun		go	do			Gun		go	do		
Pattern 2	Gun		go	do	go	do	Gun			X		
Pattern 3	Gun		go	do	go	do	Gun		go	do		
Pattern 4	Gun		go	do	go	do	Gun		pa			
Pattern 5	Gun		go	do	go	do	Gun		pa	ta		
Pattern 6	Gun		go	do	go	do	Gun	pa	go	pa	go	
XP	Gun	go	do	Gun	go	do	Gun	go	do	Gun	go	do

X = clap, XP = cross pattern

Here is an example with Pattern 1:

Baba's Rhythmic Pattern with the Cross Pattern											
Vocables	Ga	Ma	La	Ga	Ma	La	Ga	Ma	La	Ga	Ma	La
Time	1	2	3	1	2	3	1	2	3	1	2	3
Pattern 1	Gun		go	do			Gun		go	do		
Drum	Gun	go	do	Gun	go	do	Gun	go	do	Gun	go	do

In order to feel this little timing gem, speak the *Gun go do's* and grunt for the spaces: *Gun* (*ungh*) *go do* (*ungh ungh*).

The important thing about *speaking* the spaces with an *ungh* is for you to *feel* what is between the notes. You can *see* the spaces if you watch your hands while playing the cross pattern and speaking Pattern 1.

Pay particular attention to Patterns 4 and 6. Number 4 gives you three beats at the end that you have to account for before you begin the pattern again.

Pattern 4											
Vocables	Ga	Ma	La	Ga	Ma	La	Ga	Ma	La	Ga	Ma	La
Time	1	2	3	1	2	3	1	2	3	1	2	3
Pattern 4	Gun		go	do	go	do	Gun		pa			
XP	Gun	go	do	Gun	go	do	Gun	go	do	Gun	go	do

And Pattern 6 gives you only one beat. So there can be a feeling of having to rush into the pattern again.

Pattern 6											
Vocables	Ga	Ma	La	Ga	Ma	La	Ga	Ma	La	Ga	Ma	La
Time	1	2	3	1	2	3	1	2	3	1	2	3
Pattern 6	Gun		go	do	go	do	Gun	pa	go	pa	go	
XP	Gun	go	do	Gun	go	do	Gun	go	do	Gun	go	do

Both are really good examples for learning to feel the interval in rhythmic patterns.

Practice with a friend. See if one of you can play the cross pattern while the other plays Baba's patterns 1 through 6. See how the cross pattern (XP) can act like a metronome, to keep you grounded in the events and intervals of this exercise. Make this a part of your basic warm-up repertoire.

In YOUR Body!

The exercises given in this book offer different ways of approaching learning. You can find the rhythm in the body through stepping, using rhythm syllables, or playing your drum while stepping, or you can sit with the drum and have your hands connect to the drum language: *Gun, go do* and *pa ta*. In this chapter I'm talking about learning through stepping and getting the rhythm into your whole body.

Each subdivision of rhythms (two, three, four,) has a different feeling or temperament. The following exercises help to understand the flowing feeling of three. This is a great exercise to do after you learn to play the cross pattern in Two Becomes Three (page 38).

1. Guide yourself into a feeling of three in your steps

Imagine you are standing on a big drum. In stepping you can visualize the drum beneath you resonating. Imagine that as each step goes down there is a "boom" on that drum beneath you! You can feel the rhythm through your feet and the movement of your body.

Begin walking in place. Start your first step on your dominant side.

- Feel the two sides of the body—dominant and non-dominant. Notice what makes it possible for you to shift your body weight from one side to the other. (One side of the body takes the weight. Then shift through the center to the other side.)

- Using the rhythm syllables, call the dominant side *Ta* and the non-dominant, *Ki*, or if you prefer 1 and 2. Continue walking back and forth in place. Eventually, bring the 3 into your voice with the syllables *Ga Ma La* or *one*, two, three. Notice that *one* occurs first with the right foot and then with the left foot! Just as you did with your hands, step forward slightly so your feet will now inscribe a triangle.

Start moving slowly. Feel the placement of each footstep, the rocking forward and the step back. Speak each footstep with the rhythm syllables or make up three sounds on your own, such as: "Here. I. Am."

Make an inner picture or map of your movement. See each footstep in its unique position.

2. Shift the awareness away from the one with the three rhythmic elements

Start speaking all of the elements of three—in *TaKeTiNa* language, *Ga Ma La*.

- Call the *La*—the element farthest away from the *one*.
- Return to singing all three of the elements in their order: *Ga Ma La*. This is to ground you before you explore the next element.
- Call the *Ma* right after the *one*. Return to singing all three of the elements in their order: *Ga Ma La*.
- Call the *Ga*. Return to singing all three of the elements in their order: *Ga Ma La*.
- Again, call the *La* —the element **before** the *one*. Return to singing all three of the elements in their order: *Ga Ma La*.

Observe what elements throw you out of rhythm. Have fun with losing your place!

Gradually, return your awareness to the three steps. Slowly, pick up your pace. Stay with your inner map, and see how quickly you can allow your feet to go. Feel each note going down into the big drum beneath your feet. See if there is a way to make your movement fluid. Loosen your head, neck, arms and shoulders, legs and hips, ankles and feet, tongue and belly.

Stay with the voice and movements. Can you still find the offbeats of *Ma* and *La* and speak them?

Gradually begin to slow your vocal pattern and body movement. Bring yourself into a more receptive listening and feeling mode as you allow your movements to become less and less visible and auditory.

Gradually sit down or lie down, close your eyes, and direct your attention inward. Feel into the body. What do you sense?

Dance and Drum

I loved the feeling of unity and power in playing together with the group in Baba's classes. He knew how to build a container of energy and sound. Whether he was with fifty people or a thousand, Baba had this way that he could hold the energy in the room and make you feel like he was speaking to you, only you!

Each day, each class, for the first hour and a half, we began with Baba teaching drumming. The remainder of the class was dance. We had men and women teachers, and each expressed a different aspect of the music.

The choreography in Baba's class, based in isolative movements, was a great way to enter African dance. The drum music becomes the vehicle you ride! Once you remember the steps and movements, the dance expresses the meaning of the rhythm with your whole being.

Dancing to good drum music is not only great exercise…it's sexy, sweaty and fun! The joy doesn't diminish, it just gets better as you incorporate the dance and drum rhythms.

Dance and Drum are One

I believe, as Baba did, that dancing is essential for drummers. In many cultures drum and dance are inseparable. For example, in the Congolese drum and dance camp, *hundreds* of dancers attend classes. The male dancers on the floor are also good drummers. In West African Malinke drumming, the lead drummers learn solos that illustrate the dancers' steps. In the Kathak dance of southern India, the dancer recites *bols*—the rhythmic pattern that he or she will dance and the *tabla* drummer will play. The dance is the visual display of the unity of dancer and drummer.

Understanding from experience how the dance and drum are united gives you another skill in becoming a valuable drummer. When you can dance to the music yourself, your understanding of the feeling in the body translates back to your playing on the drum. You begin to serve the music for a purpose greater than just playing for fun. You serve the dance, the visual expression of rhythm.

The Dancers Feed the Drummers

If you are connected to what the dancers are doing in their movements, your drumming has a visual context. You see the rhythm in feet, hands, hips, shoulders, and heads. Seeing the rhythm in motion helps you understand the *phrasing* inside the drum parts. The energy that the dancers bring to the floor encourages you when you are tiring from playing the same rhythm for an hour. You are important to the dance! You can see how you contribute to the living art before you.

When I played in Baba's classes, there was always a moment when I would begin to run out of steam. Shifting my focus from my tiredness to whoever was on the floor and realizing that they needed my energy would help to pump me up again.

The Drummers Feed the Dancers

Listening to the drum can inspire and fuel your movements. The drum is telling you how to dance, what tempo, and when to change your step. It is feeding you energy, it is telling you about your hand movements and footsteps. It is encouraging you to go deeper inside the music and the movement.

Playing the drum or dancing in a field of unity is magic, powerful and uplifting. If you did not believe in God, the music and the joy could make a believer out of you. (See Alalade Frederick's interview, page 100.)

Developing Focus

The development of focus is an important aspect of drumming. Focus allows drum songs to develop, engage the listeners, and encourage dance or movement from the audience. The exercises that can aid in developing mastery—from yoga to cooking, mechanics to meditation—all require focus, but a soft, persuasive, gentle focus.

Focus is an interior process one can *willfully and intentionally* develop (but not by straining). It is a happy by-product of bringing presence to rhythm and life. When we relax deeply inside rhythm, our sense of time and space expands.

You can *intend* to focus and relax into the rhythm. And you can actively move into the rhythm with your awareness. Imagine being present with every note that you play. No spacing out. Rhythm demands your participation. It is *this* sound here and now, hear and now.

By developing focus through drumming, we expand our capacity to listen to others. Any musical communication is more likely to land if we are in the moment. Dialogue in music can come from space and time instead of stress and ego.

Here are some suggestions to encourage focus:
- Soft eyes—allowing the visual field to broaden, being aware of the periphery, what is above and below.
- Awareness of breath—inhalation and exhalation—feeling the relaxation of the belly with the breath. Relax your belly, relax your jaw. (See Visualization for Chi, page 86.)
- Mindfulness and body awareness—sitting up straight and feeling supported by your spine.
- Repeating the mantra; whether it is drum rhythms or rhythm meditation syllables (or vocables), keep speaking them to stay focused on what you are playing.
- Enjoy yourself! Allow micro-movements that allow the hands to dance on the head of the drum, while in larger body movements notice how the feet connect with the floor.
- Develop a practice—five minutes, three times a week (see How to Practice with the Drum, page 27). Practice doesn't make perfect, it makes practice.

As you continue to focus your awareness, your capacity to focus grows. At some point you are not trying so hard. You arrive here and now. All you are doing is breathing, moving, riding the wave of attention, and refreshing your sense of the moment through your breath. We do have limits, physically, for how long we can play, but not for focus. It is important to recognize false emotional or psychological limits that we buy into. And the enemy of all: boredom.

You need a few things to help you gain focus:
- Posture
- Breathing
- Technique
- Momentum
- Listen

Always Switch Parts

You will find, as you continue building your song and drum repertoire, that there are certain songs or rhythms that you love, that your body loves and understands, and that stick to you.

You may understand others less clearly, feel vague about the timing, or have trouble remembering how the parts intersect. Then there are others that you don't like very much at all. Sorry. Learn to play all the parts. Enjoy all the parts!

Sometimes, in class or at a workshop, we divvy up the parts for a rhythmic orchestration ("who wants to play part 1? 2?" etc.) There are always those who wait and wait and wait. Maybe they are looking for a more perfect part or *only, always,* want to play the top part.

It's great to play the top part. Usually that is the part where you have to get your chops going. (Your chops—that's like, your skills, technique, and focus. Have you got the chops to play this? Yah!) The top is juicy. But it's not all there. No Way!

I play the top sometimes because I can. I understand the phrasing, the way the rhythm sounds *connected* to the bottom. But I play the bottom really well, too.

Is it annoying to play the bottom when you know you can play the top better than the person who is playing it? Yes and no.

For the ego it is irritating, chafing.

But for the one who serves the music, it is what it is—an opportunity to use the bottom to build a really great orchestration.

Remember, there are no small parts, just small people! It's like the joke about the neophyte actor who gets his first small non-speaking part. He is supposed to walk on the stage, put the tea service on the table, and walk out. He tells his mother that he just landed his first part, and she asks, "Well, darling, what is the play about?" He answers proudly, "It is about a butler who serves tea."

The point is, although you may want more recognition, the part you are playing is still the most important part in the room!

⊚

Play with the Other Hand

The first time I injured my body in a drumming-related way, I was lucky to have a physical therapist who was familiar with the body mechanics involved in hand drumming. After assessing my injury and range of motion she said casually, "Oh, so you play with your right hand." I asked her how she knew.

She said, "Your trapezius is very well developed on your right side, and undeveloped on your left. You obviously favor your right side when playing."

Uh-oh. I was caught! I was always putting off re-learning *Gun, go* and *pa* with my non-dominant side. I had been feeling competent playing with my right hand. I didn't want to have to go into a learning curve again! But why put off the inevitable? Using both sides of your body means stimulating both sides of your brain. And that has to be good for us, especially as we get older.

I remember watching Baba continuing to develop his technique on his left hand—and encouraging everyone else to do the same.

Aside from practicing rhythms with your non-dominant side, there are a couple of exercises that are good for switching your lead.

Exercise 1: Switch Leading Hand																
Vocables	Ta	Ke	Ti	Na	Ta	Ke	Ti	Na	Ta	Ke	Ti	Na	Ta	Ke	Ti	Na
Time	1	2	3	4	1	2	3	4	1	2	3	4	1	2	3	4
Drum	pa		ta		go		do		pa		ta		go	do	go	
Hand	R		L		R		L		R		L		R	L	R	
		L		R		L		R		L		R		L	R	L

Notice in the chart that the leading hand is first on the right side, and then the left hand leads! Try to increase your speed as you become more and more comfortable with switching your lead hand in this rhythm.

Paradiddles

A paradiddle consists of alternating right and left hand and then adding a double hit on the right or left hand. Learn to switch your lead hand RLRR or LRLL. This is a great exercise for increasing speed and the ability to shift from your dominant to non-dominant hand.

Exercise 2: Paradiddles							
R	L	R	R	L	R	L	L
go	do	go	go	do	go	do	do

Shifting Awareness Away from the *One*:
Learning the Elements of Three

When we initially learn to drum, we focus on posture, how to play notes, remembering rhythms, learning to play in an ensemble. We also explore rhythmic structures, events, and spaces. Exercises such as Learning the Flow in Four (page 19) help in experiencing each beat within a four-beat cycle.

And yet, sometimes the question arises: Why do I need to learn about rhythm? I just want to play the drum!

I think that a musician learning what is inside a rhythm is like an artist learning about the colors on a color wheel. Mixing colors can change mood, shading, and depth in a piece of art. In the same way, the elements within a rhythmic pattern inform how we feel in our bodies, how drum patterns influence us.

This next exercise gives an opportunity once again to enjoy the process of falling out of rhythm. Don't make a big deal about it. You will fall out, even if you know where the beat is and should be. The point is to continue to practice finding the elements in a rhythm until your perception of space (or interval) is as clear as your awareness of beat!

Start speaking all of the elements of three—in drum language or vocables, *Gun go do* or *Ga Ma La*, using the cross pattern again to become more aware of these elements. Your hands will be in an ongoing pattern that enables you to see-feel the position of the hands in relation to the notes.

Finding the Elements of Three

See video: www.WholePersonDrummingBook.com (Elements of Three).

1. Call the *La* or the *do*

The element farthest away from the *one*. Try to see where your hands are on the drum for the off-beat *La* or *do*. Call *La* when you see your hand playing the *La* or *do*. Finally, return to singing all three of the elements in their order—*Ga Ma La*—*Gun go do*—to ground yourself before moving forward (or backward).

2. Call the *Ma* or *go* right after the *one*

Return to singing all three of the elements in their order: *Ga Ma La*. See the *Ma* hand on the drum. Hear yourself speak *Ma* at the moment that you feel the hand touch the drumhead. Sing some *Ma*-oriented songs like: *(ungh) Ma La Ga Ma La*. Return to singing—*Gun go do*.

3. Call the *Ga* or *Gun*

Return to singing all of three of the elements in their order: *Ga Ma La, Gun go do*. See your hands moving in the shape of a triangle. Find a song that pleases you. Enjoy your melodies and experimentation. Enjoy hearing the rhythm for the *one* once again. And finally…

4. Call the *La* before the *one*

The element farthest away from the *one*—before the *one*! This is a great moment to feel the pull of the *one* as you inhabit a space (place) before it. Return to singing all three of the elements in their order: *Ga Ma La* or *Gun go do*.

Here's the exercise (also remember Two Becomes Three on page 38):

	Elements of Three					
Vocables	Ga	Ma	La	Ga	Ma	La
Drum	Gun	go	do	Gun	go	do
Hand	R	L	R	L	R	L
1 call:			La			La
Return to:	Ga	Ma	La	Ga	Ma	La
2 call		Ma			Ma	
Return to:	Ga	Ma	La	Ga	Ma	La
3 call	Ga			Ga		
Return to:	Ga	Ma	La	Ga	Ma	La
4 call: *La*			La			
Return to:	Ga	Ma	La	Ga	Ma	La

Observe what elements throw you out of rhythm. Have fun losing your place!

As we end this exercise, please begin by softening the voice and the drum through making smaller movements and having less volume in your voice. As we bring the music softer and softer, it can sound like a melody being carried off into the distance. As we open our listening, we can hear how that rhythm begins to become louder *inside* us at the same time that the sound becomes less audible externally, as in Fadeout (page 71).

Continue following the softening audible sound and the growing internal sound. This is how the experience of music goes from something publicly heard to an internal sense of melody and rhythm that grows as the external cues begin to fade away.

Single and Double Time Exercises

Drumming includes many skills: learning rhythms, coordination of technique, and drum orchestration, to name a few. Included in this list of important qualities is understanding and becoming friends with intervals in time, or the spaces between the notes. (I keep saying that, don't I?) A skillful use of time and space is one of the necessities to encourage the god/goddess *groove* to come out of his/her den.

When intervals are respected and tempo has settled, a drummer, musician, communicator, can hear when they can interject a pleasing piece of new information into the whole/hole. But what can you play?

Understanding single time and double time can be your ally in expressing tasty bits of sound.

Here is a simple exercise that you can do with the drum and finally with your whole body!

Start this exercise sitting down. Once again we'll start with the subdivision of three, or the cross pattern (also found on page 38).

Speak the single time, which is what you are playing on the drum. Notice that your hands are always changing: right left right, and left right left: *Gun go do, Gun go do*. As you feel comfortable playing the pattern, play *while bringing your voice into double time*.

Notice that the first *Gun* and the third *Gun* line up with the right hand or left hand.

Eventually change your *playing* to the double time. After that, change your *voice* to the *single time* again while playing the double time.

Then gradually change your playing back to the single time. Find this lesson at www.WholePerson DrummingBook.com (Single Time Double Time).

Switch back and forth until going from single time to double time gets easier and easier.

Single Time						
Speak	Ga	Ma	La	Ga	Ma	La
Time	1	2	3	1	2	3
Drum	Gun	go	do	Gun	go	do
Hand	R	L	R	L	R	L

Double Time												
Speak	Ga	Ma	La	Ga	Ma	La	Ga	Ma	La	Ga	Ma	La
Time	1	2	3	1	2	3	1	2	3	1	2	3
Drum	Gun	go	do	Gun	go	do	Gun	go	do	Gun	go	do
* Step	R						L					

*Challenging!

Now that you have learned this pattern, let's include the steps! See them at the bottom of the chart above.

Stand with your drum, either by putting on straps, putting the drum on a chair with bungee cords or ropes, or using a stand for your instrument.

This is how to build this journey into time, space, and movement. For each *Gun* that you play, step with alternating feet. (I indicated right foot first, because many more of my students are right dominant.) Notice what it is like to enter into movement. You can feel the interval (*go do*) between each footstep.

As you get more and more comfortable with the steps and the voice being together, switch your voice to the double time.

Notice the first and third *Gun* in your voice on the footstep. Feel the spaciousness between your footsteps as you play in double time. Allow yourself to fluctuate between the *single time* and *double time* on the drum, while your steps stay in the *single time*.

Eventually you can include exercises that identify and include all the elements in the *double time*. You can call all the *Gun's* (*Ga's*), *go's* (*Ma's*), and *do's* (*La's*). Challenging and fun!

Increase Your Speed and Stamina

As I have noted before, technique, or the ability to replicate and make clear, consistent sounds of the notes on the drum is an important part of your drum training.

The next challenge is to be able to increase your speed while you play precisely! This helps build upper body strength and increases your stamina to play for longer periods of time without getting enervated.

Twelve-Beat Cycle

Try the exercise below. It is a simple twelve-beat cycle. As you play faster, give yourself the space to rest and relax while you increase the tempo. The four *Gun's* in Part 2 allow you to rest while building tolerance for playing at higher tempos. Part 1 is the cross pattern—crossing the mid-line. The cross pattern is a great rhythm for so many things, including building strength.

Cross Pattern with *Guns*												
Vocables	Ga	Ma	La	Ga	Ma	La	Ga	Ma	La	Ga	Ma	La
Time	1	2	3	1	2	3	1	2	3	1	2	3
Part 1	Gun	go	do	Gun	go	do	Gun	go	do	Gun	go	do
Part 2	Gun			Gun			Gun			Gun		

Start with four *Gun go do's*. Follow with four *Gun's* ONLY. (Part 2 keeps the space where the *go do's* would be.)

This exercise allows you to rest, play all the notes, then rest again! It also allows you to hear the difference in your right and left playing of the same notes. You can change this exercise to start with your non-dominant hand.

Flow

Here is little workout with two different subdivisions in a cycle of twelve beats altogether. The first subdivision is two or *Ta Ki*. To make 12, there are six *Ta Ki's*. The second subdivision is three, or *Ga Ma La*. Because the common denominator is 12, we will have four threes or *Ga Ma La's*.

Practice Part 1 four times and then Part 2 four times. Alternate!

Flow												
Vocables	*Ta*	*Ki*	*Ta*	*Ki*	*Ta*	*Ki*	*Ta*	*Ki*	*Ta*	*Ki*	*Ta*	*Ki*
Time	1	2	1	2	1	2	1	2	1	2	1	2
Hand	R	L	R	L	R	L	R	L	R	L	R	L
Part 1	Gun	Gun	go	do	pa	ta	Gun	Gun	go	do	pa	ta
Part 2	pa	ta	go	do	Gun	Gun	pa	ta	go	do	Gun	Gun

This is another kind of flow exercise that allows you to move back and forth from the center to the sides, from *go do* (tones) to *pa ta* (slaps). Concentrate on saying the notes as you play them. Pick up your speed until the notes sound mushy, then go back to playing slowly.

All these exercises can help to build speed and stamina.

Eight-Beats with Technique							
Ta	*Ke*	*Ti*	*Na*	*Ta*	*Ke*	*Ti*	*Na*
1	2	3	4	1	2	3	4
Gun	Gun	go	do	Gun	Gun	pa	ta

chapter four

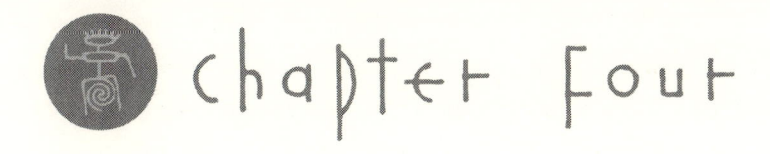

Rhythms That Rock!
Root Rhythms

Since, as I've discussed in the chapter on Learning Styles, I discovered in my teaching that we all learn in our own time, I wondered if there might be a root phrase, an essential part of any rhythm that is easy enough for anyone to play. There often is. I started to notice these root phrases.

If you can play the root phrase, you don't have to play all the parts immediately. You can join in and be part of a group playing more complex parts while you hold onto the basic groove.

Here is one root rhythm plus variations, or accompaniments, that together make up an orchestration or a song of Congolese 4/4 rhythms. We could call this first rhythm the "bottom" part of this Congolese 4/4 composition. It's the core of the composition. The bottom can exist on its own, but there can't be a top without a bottom! It's like a cake—there can't be icing without the cake.

The root is **Part 1**: This is the simple 4/4 rhythm that I describe in Beginning Practice, Beginning Rhythms (page 33).

Root Rhythms: Part 1															
Ta	Ke	Ti	Na	Ta	Ke	Ti	Na	Ta	Ke	Ti	Na	Ta	Ke	Ti	Na
1	2	3	4	1	2	3	4	1	2	3	4	1	2	3	4
Gun		go		Gun				Gun		go		Gun			

Now I'm going to show you some accompaniments to the root rhythm that make up a "family" of Congolese 4/4 rhythms all derived from this one root. Your ability to play this one simple song repeatedly maximizes your potential for learning, understanding, and remembering all the other rhythms in this orchestration. This one rhythm (part 1) is a sound bite as opposed to a phrase. The phrase is demonstrated in part 2 of this orchestration.

The *Gun* is played with the dominant hand. The *go* is played with the non-dominant hand.

This simple pattern offers the opportunity for drummers in any group to build up momentum, a container for groove to arrive. It allows you to be present in an engaged way. This rhythm (and the cross pattern found on page 38) is great to allow you to stay focused and serve the music.

Part 2 shows the root rhythm in a context where it repeats into a phrase or a "story." It has a beginning, middle, and end. Whenever a phrase is set up in a rhythmic context with other orchestrated rhythms, that phrase becomes the definition of the largest cycle of that rhythmic orchestration. In other words, there are four of Part 1 within every Part 2.

Root Rhythms: Part 2															
Ta	Ke	Ti	Na	Ta	Ke	Ti	Na	Ta	Ke	Ti	Na	Ta	Ke	Ti	Na
1	2	3	4	1	2	3	4	1	2	3	4	1	2	3	4
Gun		go		Gun				Gun		go		Gun			
Gun		go		Gun		Gun		Gun		go		Gun			

Part 3 shown on following page, has a mnemonic that can help you remember the pattern. Each syllable or word goes on a note. It goes like this: *rhy-thm-rhy-thm-I've-got-the-rhy-thm*.

Two complete phrases of Part 3 equal one "story" of Part 2. We still have the theme of dominant hand leading with the *Gun* and non-dominant playing the *go's*.

We are also playing the more difficult offbeats with the non-dominant hand.

						Root Rhythms: Part 3									
Ta	Ke	Ti	Na	Ta	Ke	Ti	Na	Ta	Ke	Ti	Na	Ta	Ke	Ti	Na
1	2	3	4	1	2	3	4	1	2	3	4	1	2	3	4
R		L		R		L		R	L		L	R		L	
Gun		go		Gun		go		Gun	go		go	Gun		go	
rhy		thm		rhy		thm		I've	got		the	rhy		thm	

Part 4 changes things. You play the bass note and the first tone with the same hand. By pulling your dominant hand back from the *Gun* to the *go*, you create a small circle.

I hope this shows you how you can play a simple rhythm and still be an important part of the group.

						Root Rhythms: Part 4									
Ta	Ke	Ti	Na	Ta	Ke	Ti	Na	Ta	Ke	Ti	Na	Ta	Ke	Ti	Na
1	2	3	4	1	2	3	4	1	2	3	4	1	2	3	4
Gun		go	do	Gun		go	do	Gun	go		do	Gun		go	do
R		R	L	R		R	L	R	R		L	R		R	L

Fanga

Fanga is a rhythm from Liberia, both a dance and a song. According to Baba, Fanga, the dance, was noted by members of the National Geographic Society of London when they landed in Liberia, looking for the source of the river Niger.

Pearl Primus was one of the first African-American dancers who traveled to Africa to learn traditional dances. She came back with this dance and rhythm. Baba played drums for her performance of *Fanga*. This composition later became part of his teaching curriculum for drum and dance. He added the song.

Lots of people had the experience of learning *Fanga Alafia* in grade school, during Black History month. So regardless of its true origin, here is another example of how music can teach culture and educate and inspire beyond reading, writing, and 'rithmetic. It is a wonderful rhythm and dance to learn. And here it is:

Fanga															
Vocables	*Ta*	*Ke*	*Ti*	*Na*	*Ta*	*Ke*	*Ti*	*Na*	*Ta*	*Ke*	*Ti*	*Na*	*Ta*	*Ke*	*Ti*	*Na*
Time	1	2	3	4	1	2	3	4	1	2	3	4	1	2	3	4
Bottom	Gun			go		do	go		Gun		Gun			go	do	
Top	pa	ta			pa	ta			pa	ta			pa	ta		
Part 3	Gun		Gun		Gun	go	do	Gun				Gun	go	do		
Bell			X	X		X	X			X	X				X	X

Remember the story of my "audition" with Baba? The top part of the rhythm is shown here. See how the second *pa ta* "pulls" against the rhythm.

Baya and Intervals of Four

This rhythm is awesome! This is such a cool rhythm to teach people, from beginners to advanced. You'll need four people to play this rhythm. It is a great icebreaker to use when working with new groups. I learned Baya from Sanga of the Valley. I first introduce this rhythmic phrase in Beginning Practice, Beginning Rhythms (page 33).

Baya																
Vocables	Ta	Ke	Ti	Na	Ta	Ke	Ti	Na	Ta	Ke	Ti	Na	Ta	Ke	Ti	Na
Time	1	2	3	4	1	2	3	4	1	2	3	4	1	2	3	4
Part 1	go	do	go	do	Gun	—	—	—	Gun	—	—	—	Gun	—	—	—
Part 2					go	do	go	do	Gun	—	—	—	Gun	—	—	—
	Gun	—	—	—												
Part 3									go	do	go	do	Gun	—	—	—
	Gun	—	—	—	Gun	—	—	—								
Part 4													go	do	go	do
	Gun	—	—	—	Gun	—	—	—	Gun	—	—	—				
Bell	X			X			X			X			X			

Let's analyze this rhythm. Please check out the video, **www.WholePersonDrummingBook.com** (Baya Rhythm).

Part one says: *go do go do* (or *Ta Ke Ti Na* or 1 2 3 4), followed by *Gun*—one event—with three empty cells: *go do go do Gun* space, *Gun* space, *Gun* space. After you get the rhythm song in your hands, then **speak** the syllables **in the intervals** (marked by the **dash**) and see whether you are in the pocket! You can either speak numbers (2, 3, 4), or rhythm syllables (*Ke Ti Na*), or sounds (*ungh, ungh, ungh*).

This great rhythm is played in a round (like Row, Row, Row Your Boat). Each group plays the same rhythmic pattern but *spaced* one measure apart.

Each group has to be in the same tempo in order to enter the rhythm.

It reminds me of playing jump rope when I was a kid. You have to be in synch with the beat of the rope in order to jump in. Then you have to keep the tempo in your body movement consistent so you can stay within the circle. And, you have to jump high enough so that the rope doesn't hit you on your ankles, or you're out.

Even though you're not running in the center to jump rope, playing Baya requires the same tenacity in holding onto the rhythm when you enter. If you are the first group you get to set the tempo. If you come in second, third, or fourth, listen to what the group before you is playing. Follow them—same speed, same syllables. The group behind you is depending on you to enter in place to keep the rhythm moving.

There are four parts to this round, meaning four small groups in the whole. Each of these smaller groups will have a different response to playing the rhythm. Some people in their "pod" want to enter too quickly! They are the excited ones! Some folks will enter hesitantly. Over time everyone will sense the pattern and come in in their own place.

After breaking the whole circle into four parts, I have each group enter the round with singing the pattern *before* playing it on the drum. When we get the round going vocally first, the energy is contagious. It's wonderful when this rhythm takes off. It gives each group a chance to morph into teams!

As each smaller group begins to play it, the folks in that group begin to bond. The "stronger" or more stable drummers begin to organically lead their quadrant of the circle.

Of course, there may be a train wreck or someone dropping out of their part. This is an opportunity to remember that *falling out of rhythm is a natural part of learning to drum*. The rhythm can continue as long as one small group of the four hangs in. Then the other groups can rebuild their parts quickly.

TIPS

Listen to the four voices on the video: www.WholePersonDrummingBook.com (Baya Rhythm). First focus on only getting your part right, falling into the spiraling quality of the rhythm. After a while playing together, begin to focus on the *dynamic*: How does my energy influence my small group?

Listen to the groups to modulate your volume to match theirs. Those small adjustments in volume and tension will affect the music of the whole.

This rhythm, when played over a period of time mindfully, can teach us about modulation of volume or dynamic better than anyone saying, "Shhhhhhhhhhh."

We'll return to this pattern later on when we discuss Additive Structured Eight Baya (see page 66). But this is just a teaser, of course!

Baya is a wonderful way to learn nonverbally to rely on each other and feel the rhythm carry us. We experience these moments when the magic or the groove allows us to feel the power of playing in the whole group—just being in the moment, playing our parts and feeling connected to each other.

The Bell Rules

The bell (or *gankogui* or *agogo*) is an instrument that is played with a stick. The bell plays the **clave** (clah-vay). The word clave has two meanings: one is a musical concept: a guideline, key pattern, timeline. *Clave* is a Spanish word meaning code or key, as in key to a mystery or puzzle. It's as if the clave is the skeleton and all the rhythms are the parts that flesh out the body of the music. (See also Finding the 4/4 Groove in the Body, page 22.) BUT claves are also resonant percussive sticks! So, to clarify these two terms: **The bell plays the clave (the key pattern). And claves (sticks) can also play the clave (the key pattern).**

Clave, the musical concept, also points to a musical guideline where two crosspulses or polyrhythms connect to one another to form a song. (See more on Polyrhythms page 17.)

I have heard from more than one teacher that the bell is the center of a rhythmic orchestration. I was told that if we grew up as kids in a drumming culture, we would start on the bell for the first years of playing. No drum. Just one note, learning timing and hearing all the rhythmic orchestrations. Then maybe two notes, or maybe the entire phrasing of a *bell pattern (the clave, the key).*

"How boring," says the Western mind. "I wanna play, I wanna rip it up!"

Clave sticks

The bell (or gankogui or agogo) is an instrument that is played with a stick.

If, as a child, you had played the clave or bell for different rhythms in many different drum orchestrations, it would be quite easy to switch to the drum. You would have already heard all the rhythms *clearly*, and more importantly, you would know how those rhythms interlock with each other.

Here's a great example of an easy 4/4 clave: Calypso bells. This exercise is designed to help you feel the difference between playing the bell on the beat while stepping on the beat, and playing the bell on the offbeat while continuing to step on the beat! As the bell pattern becomes more comfortable you can hear the dialogue between the beat and offbeat. Sounds awesome when played with Calypso!

Calypso Bells															
Ta	Ke	Ti	Na	Ta	Ke	Ti	Na	Ta	Ke	Ti	Na	Ta	Ke	Ti	Na
1	2	3	4	1	2	3	4	1	2	3	4	1	2	3	4
X	X			X	X			X	X			X	X		
		X	X			X	X			X	X			X	X
S				S				S				S			

S = step, X = bell

In a rhythmically intelligent world, the bell holds the whole music together. The bell expresses the guidelines of the polyrhythmic structure. It is the holder of tempo. If the bell speeds up we speed up. Period.

You can always tell the education of a drummer by how they respond to the bell. If the bell speeds up and the drummer is unaware of the power of the instrument, they continue along on their way without hearing the signal. Sooner or later the rubber hits the road and the rhythm collapses.

Cross Rhythms
or Two Ways of Looking at Eight Counts

In the world of music, cross rhythms are technically a meeting of the minds between two styles of interpreting eight counts. The two styles are called *additive and divisive cycles*. Think of a *divisive cycle* as being one where the eight counts (or two groups of four beats) are all equally divided, with the *one* having the greatest emphasis or weight.

The *additive cycle* is broken up into three, three, and two beats, adding up to eight. When you put these two patterns together, the push and pull of the *one* is what makes the rhythms interact with one another and inform the time that we hear and feel. It's groovy.

The bell plays the skeleton without any adornment. The second drum part is playing part of the clave; this shows how the offbeat and clave work and don't work together—they push and pull against each other. To play this, you'll need at least three people: two on drums and one playing the bell.

This is the *clave* of the *Bo Diddley beat* or *Not Fade Away* by Buddy Holly, later performed by the Grateful Dead. (It is also the same as the 4/4 clave used in the exercises in Finding the 4/4 Groove in the Body, page 22.)

Cross Rhythms								
Vocables	*Ta*	*Ke*	*Ti*	*Na*	*Ta*	*Ke*	*Ti*	*Na*
Time	1	2	3	4	1	2	3	4
Beat/Offbeat	*Gun*		*go*		*Gun*			
Additive	*Ga*	*Ma*	*La*	*Ga*	*Ma*	*La*	*Ta*	*Ki*
Drum	*go*	*do*		*pa*	*go*	*do*	*pa*	
Hand	R	L		L	R	L	R	
Bell	X			X			X	
			X		X			

Additive Structured Eight Baya, Top Part

As we develop as drummers we can take the simplest rhythms and make them more intricate. Baya is an example of that.

Baya, as a round, allows you to develop listening within a group, finding your place in a sequence, and developing trust in fellow drummers.

Here's how to take this simple rhythm and make it more complex. (See Baya and Intervals of Four on page 60)

Baya Basic 4 X 4 = 16 Counts																
Vocables	Ta	Ke	Ti	Na	Ta	Ke	Ti	Na	Ta	Ke	Ti	Na	Ta	Ke	Ti	Na
Time	1	2	3	4	5	6	7	8	9	10	11	12	13	14	15	16
Part 1	go	do	go	do	Gun				Gun				Gun			
	Gun															
Part 2					go	do	go	do	Gun				Gun			
	Gun				Gun											
Part 3									go	do	go	do	Gun			
	Gun				Gun											
Part 4													go	do	go	do
	Gun				Gun				Gun							

Baya becomes complex in the following way: The rhythm contains sixteen beats. In the basic rhythm it is divided up into four beats in four groups. But we can also divide it another way.

Keep the four beats at the beginning of the rhythm.

Beginning of the Baya Rhythm																
Vocables	Ta	Ke	Ti	Na												
Time	1	2	3	4	1	2	3	4	1	2	3	4	1	2	3	4
Drum	go	do	go	do												

Notice that there are twelve beats left. Divide the twelve remaining beats by four. Now the structure looks like the chart below:

Divide the Twelve Remaining Beats by Four																
Vocables	Ta	Ke	Ti	Na	Ga	La	Ma	La	Ga	La	Ma	La	Ga	La	Ma	La
Time	1	2	3	4	1	2	3	1	2	3	1	2	3	1	2	3
Drum	go	do	go	do												

Let's add the cross pattern to feel the three subdivision:

Add the Cross Pattern																
Vocables	Ta	Ki	Ti	Na	Ga	Ma	La	Ga	Ma	La	Ga	Ma	La	Ga	Ma	La
Time	1	2	3	4	1	2	3	1	2	3	1	2	3	1	2	3
Drum	go	do	go	do	Gun	go	do	Gun	go	do	Gun	go	do	Gun	go	do
Hand	R	L	R	L	R	L	R	L	R	L	R	L	R	L	R	L

Finally the true Baya top part (chart on following page). This is not an easy part to play as the *pa ta's* pull against the main pulse and each other. None of them line up with one another.

							True Baya Top Part								
Vocables	Ta	Ke	Ti	Na	Ga	Ma	La	Ga	Ma	La	Ga	Ma	La	Ga	Ma	La
Time	1	2	3	4	1	2	3	1	2	3	1	2	3	1	2	3
Part 1	go	do	go	do	pa	ta		pa	ta		pa	ta		pa	ta	
	R	L	R	L	R	L		L	R		R	L		L	R	
Part 2					go	do	go	do	pa	ta		pa	ta		pa	ta
		pa	ta													
Part 3								go	do	go	do	ta	pa			pa
	ta		pa	ta		pa	ta									
Part 4													go	do	go	do
		pa	ta		pa	ta		pa	ta		pa	ta				

To stabilize the rhythm I ask some people in each of the four groups to continue to play the bottom part of Baya, while others play the top. That way you can practice hearing the cross rhythm, or polyrhythm, of three and four played against each other.

The Break

The break is a signal, usually played by one drummer—the leader—for a designated rhythm. The signal tells other players to start or stop, or indicates other changes in the drum music. (The break is also used as a signal for dancers. The break tells dancers when to change their steps.) *Therefore, it is important to learn to hear the break as a separate and distinct signal.* Finally, the break gives intrinsic information about the tempo at which any piece is being played.

When the break is played correctly, it starts in time with the music. The break goes unnoticed by the audience, but is heard by the drummers. At the end of the break phrase, all the drummers stop playing simultaneously. The audience assumes it is the Psychic Drummers Network—but it is an embedded message.

Practice the Break with Calypso

Start with the generic 4/4 break that you hear on the video www.WholePersonDrummingBook.com (Break with Calypso Rhythm).

Calypso Bottom Part with Break Pattern																
Vocables	Ta	Ke	Ti	Na	Ta	Ke	Ti	Na	Ta	Ke	Ti	Na	Ta	Ke	Ti	Na
Double time	1	2	3	4	1	2	3	4	1	2	3	4	1	2	3	4
Single time	1		2		3		4		1		2		3		4	
Step	R		L		R		L		R		L		R		L	
Drum	Gun			Gun	Gun		go		Gun			Gun	Gun		go	
Break	go		do		go		do	go			do		go			

Step = Training Wheels step, Drum = pattern for Calypso bottom, Break pattern

Learn it. Play it in your mind, and also sing it. On the chart below, the Calypso bottom part (*Gun - - Gun Gun - go*) is played twice to match the sixteen beats of the break.

After you memorize the melody of the break you can internalize it further by stepping the pattern while you play the drum.

This is a way you can play the break using your body awareness.

- Stand and find the pulse in your body, by **speaking** *Ta Ke Ti Na* or counting one two three four. Gently begin to emphasize the syllables *Ta* and *Ti* or 1 and 3 (Training Wheels).

- Begin to **step** the rhythm using the right foot (or your dominant foot) as the **one** or **Ta** and left foot as the **three** or **Ti**.

- When you are comfortable in your step, **speak** the *Calypso* rhythm **while stepping**. Continue to feel the rhythm while speaking the pattern, until you can feel or sense where the notes land with your footsteps (marked in gray).

- Now work with a partner. One of you continues speaking the Calypso rhythm while stepping. The other partner will begin to sing the **break** on top of the drum pattern while mirroring the same step. You will notice that two of the drum patterns equal one entire break!

After you have taken turns to find the break pattern through stepping, then take a seat and begin to play the pattern of the Calypso bottom part on the drum.

Practice the Break

In a group or alone, try to speak the break while playing the Calypso bottom. If this feels out of your reach right now, no worries. Either have a recording of the Calypso rhythm playing OR have your friends or folks in class play the Calypso rhythm while you stop playing. Tune in to where the Calypso bottom pattern begins and ends. When you can allow yourself to relax, see if you can speak the break over the drums or your recording. Then try to play the break. Enjoy the opportunity to allow two rhythmic messages to speak at the same time!

After you feel more familiar with playing the break try this exercise

Play the rhythm, then play the break, stop the music, count to four and come in again with the bottom to Calypso.

You want to be able to *internalize* the music you are playing. The development of an internal recording of the music allows you to relax more deeply into feeling where to begin to play the break.

Another exercise

Play the calypso bottom and have each person in a group take a turn (or more than one turn) playing the break, counting to four, and returning to the bottom. If you come in late or early or forget the break pattern, keep trying. Learning to play the break increases the chances of hearing the break when someone else plays it!

Fadeout

The break is a way to end a piece of music that can create some surprise or excitement. The music is playing and then all of a sudden it ends! Sometimes there is an *orchestrated* break for the entire group of drummers, as in the Rock Rhythm (page 72), where the group plays the break *together* to start the rhythm and to end it as well.

There are other ways to end a drum orchestration. One is the fadeout. The fadeout is magical. It allows the listener to experience the music more personally as it ends. We go from normal volume to gradually playing softer and softer. As the music softens, it draws the audience into listening more and more intently.

As volume decreases, our hearing begins to become more active. We make up for the lack of volume in the outside by activating the music within us. We hear the music louder on the inside as it gets quieter and quieter on the outside. By the time the music has disappeared from the audible realm it is living inside us more directly!

Experiment with the fadeout. It is a lovely way to create mood, and to gently take us all, listeners and performers, into a much more intimate space. Take your time going from fully hearing the sounds to gradually fading out.

Try it for yourself. Play a rhythm you love softer and softer until it is just your fingertips on the drum. Allow all your movements to become smaller and smaller, until you're making only a whisper. When you finish playing, close your eyes and notice your interior world. Is the rhythm still present? How do you feel?

Rock Rhythm

Here is Baba's "Rock Rhythm." You can hear the rhythm in his song *Ife Loju L'aiye*, a tribute to love—indiscriminate love. "I say love, you say love, we say love," from Baba's 1989 album, *The Beat*. You could say this is Baba's version of rock and roll. This rhythm offers a great opportunity for a group to learn to play a break (The Break, page 68) together. Here the break is part of the drum orchestration.

This is another rhythm where the *one* or the initial pulse of the rhythm and the beginning of the rhythm differ. We begin Part 1 with the *pa ta* before the *one*. Part 2 is a continuation of Part 1 with one additional *pa ta*. It is like a run-on sentence that keeps going and going. And going.

						Rock Rhythm										
Vocables	*Ta*	*Ke*	*Ti*	*Na*	*Ta*	*Ke*	*Ti*	*Na*	*Ta*	*Ke*	*Ti*	*Na*	*Ta*	*Ke*	*Ti*	*Na*
Time	1	2	3	4	1	2	3	4	1	2	3	4	1	2	3	4
Break 3x	go		do	go		do	go		go		do		go			
Break	go		do	go		do	go		Gun		Gun		pa	ta		
	Gun															
Part 1															(pa	ta)
Drum	Gun		Gun		pa	ta			Gun						(pa	ta)
Part 2													pa	ta	pa	ta
	Gun		Gun		pa	ta			Gun		pa	ta			pa	ta
Part 3	Gun		Gun		pa	ta			Gun		Gun		pa	ta		
Var.	Gun		Gun		pa	ta	pa	ta	Gun		Gun		pa	ta		
Break 3x	go		do	go		do	go		go		do		go			
Break	go		do	go		do	go		Gun		Gun		pa	ta!		

Part 3 is a bass background beat. It reminds me of a low-rider car. You can hear it several blocks before you actually see it —big bass notes that drive the rhythm!

Notice the difference between the break in the beginning of the orchestration and the break at the end. The last break has no *Gun*, leaving the listener with a sense of surprise.

Because of all the *pa ta's,* this rhythm does rock. Enjoy it at higher tempos!

Samba

I learned this Samba orchestration from Sanga of the Valley. Over time I added a few other parts that came to me from other sources. Once again I remind you that these orchestrations are adapted traditional rhythms. They allow anyone to be able to play them easily, making great music happen!

Samba Orchestration

Parts 1 and 2 are interesting rhythms to play. They have a challenge in them not because of complexity but because of the amount of *space* between the notes. However, they are easier rhythms to sing with, because the song is always on the *one* of the rhythm structure. You can end the song on the last note notated OR arch it over the measure. The song goes *ba ba la ba si le*. It is a great opportunity for call and response.

Remember, it's important to sing and play the drum together, and much easier to sing and play on parts one and two:

Samba																
Vocables	Ta	Ke	Ti	Na	Ta	Ke	Ti	Na	Ta	Ke	Ti	Na	Ta	Ke	Ti	Na
Time	1	2	3	4	1	2	3	4	1	2	3	4	1	2	3	4
Part 1	Gun				go				Gun			do	go	do		
Song	ba		ba		la		ba		si		le					
Part 2	Gun		go	do					Gun		go	do				
Drum	Gun		go	do			Gun		Gun		go	do				

Simple Samba Orchestration

Vocables	Ti	Na	Ta	Ke	Ti	Na	Ta	Ke	Ti	Na	Ta	Ke	Ti	Na	Ta	Ke	Ti	Na
Time	3	4	1	2	3	4	1	2	3	4	1	2	3	4	1	2	3	4
Part 1			Gun			go		Gun						do	go	do		
Part 2			Gun		go	do					Gun			go	do			
			Gun		go	do			Gun		Gun			go	do			
Song			ba		ba		la		ba		si		le					
Part 3	Gun	Gun	Gun		go	do	go		Gun	Gun		Gun		do	go			
Part 4			pa		pa		go	do		ta		ta		go	do	go	do	
Part 5		pa	go	do	go	do	go		pa	go	do	go	do	go				
		pa	go	do	go	pa	go	do	go	pa	go	do	go	do	go			
		pa	go	do	go	do	go	pa		pa	go	do	go	do	go			

Part 3 is a flow part. Once you learn the notes the flow happens, going back and forth from the *Gun*'s to the *go-do*'s. Note that part three starts with two pick-up notes (*Ti Na*).

Samba Part 3

Part 3	Gun	Gun	Gun		go	do	go		Gun	Gun		Gun	do	go
Hand	R	L	R		R	L	R		R	L		L	L	R

Part 3 flow also has an unusual hand pattern, the pattern that is grayed out on the chart. I call it "skippy hands" because of the double (or in this case triple) hit with one hand.

Part 4 is a song that is familiar to the samba groove. I love this accompaniment because you switch playing your slaps from your dominant to your non-dominant side. Again you can see the double and triple hits, which I have grayed out.

Part 5 starts on the four (or *na*) before the *one*. It has three variations. All of them are great for accenting the *pa* before the *one*.

Break This is a break I made up. I hope you like it.

Break																			
Ti	*Na*	*Ta*	*Ke*	*Ti*	*Na*	*Ta*	*Ke*	*Ti*	*Na*	*Ta*	*Ke*	*Ti*	*Na*	*Ta*	*Ke*	*Ti*	*Na*	*Ta*	*Ke*	*Ti*	*Na*
		go	do	go		go	do	go		go	do	go		go		do		go		do

Samba Bells The bell parts in this orchestration are a conversation. Try them out. The last two bell parts are something I cooked up.

Samba Bells																	
Vocables	Ti	Na	Ta	Ke	Ti	Na	Ta	Ke	Ti	Na	Ta	Ke	Ti	Na	Ta	Ke	Ti	Na
Time	1	2	3	4	1	2	3	4	1	2	3	4	1	2	3	4	1	2
Part 1			l		l			h	h		l		l		h	h	h	h
Part 2	(h)		h			l	l			h	h			l	l		(h)	
Part 3			h	l		h	l		h	l		l	l		h		h	
Part 4			l	h		l	h		l	h		h	h		l		l	

l = low bell, h = upper bell, on *gankogui* bells, shown in The Bell Rules on page 63

Kpanlogo *(The k is silent. Say "pan-logo.")*

I learned Kpanlogo (an adapted version of this rhythm) from Kofi Missisou in Ghana. It is important to note that I do not teach this on traditional *kpanlogo* drums, with a Ghanaian slap. Instead I have changed the slaps to *pa* and *ta*, our basic technique. Start with the bottom rhythm. Within the bottom rhythm is a small challenge: the last *pa ta*. The bottom rhythm can be taught and/or learned in two ways.

Part 1 shows the rhythm the way I originally learned it.

Part 1a introduces the "last" *pa ta* at the <u>beginning</u> of the rhythm. It seems easier for people to learn this way, because we swing into it with pick-up notes. Notice through the shading that the *pa ta*'s are the same, just positioned differently.

Part 2 of the rhythm is important. When we sing <u>on</u> the *Gun's*, this rhythm becomes stabilized and easy to sing on with no excuse! Sing and play.

Kpanlogo Drum Parts																		
Vocables	Ti	Na	Ta	Ke	Ti	Na	Ta	Ke	Ti	Na	Ta	Ke	Ti	Na	Ta	Ke	Ti	Na
Time	3	4	1	2	3	4	1	2	3	4	1	2	3	4	1	2	3	4
Part 1			go		go		Gun		pa	ta	go	do	go	do	Gun		pa	ta
Part 1a	pa	ta	go		go		Gun		pa	ta	go	do	go	do	Gun		pa	ta
Part 2	go	do	Gun		pa	ta	Gun		go	do	Gun		pa	ta	Gun		go	do

After establishing the bottom or foundation of the rhythm, we will add other parts. One is the bell pattern. The second is the song. These new additions can be challenging for a beginner; where the clave lands in relation to our perception of the *one* can tweak the mind. However, just think of it like an opera—things make their own sense in terms of their exits and entrances. Songs can start in different places and make beautiful melodies.

The rhythm can begin anywhere as long it follows the rules within the rhythm itself: the tempo stays the same, and the polyrhythmic cycle remains the same.

The song and the clave start where the darker gray line shows in the chart below. Notice how the song "punctuates" in the same place (very light gray) as the clave.

						Kpanlogo Drum, Clave, and Song												
Vocables	Ti	Na	Ta	Ke	Ti	Na	Ta	Ke	Ti	Na	Ta	Ke	Ti	Na	Ta	Ke	Ti	Na
Time	3	4	1	2	3	4	1	2	3	4	1	2	3	4	1	2	3	4
Part 1			go		go		Gun		pa	ta	go	do	go	do	Gun		pa	ta
Part 1a	pa	ta	go		go		Gun		pa	ta	go	do	go	do	Gun		pa	ta
Part 2	go	do	Gun		pa	ta	Gun		go	do	Gun		pa	ta	Gun		go	do
Clave					X		X				X			X			X	
Song											ba		ba		ba		ba	
				she	ba		ba		a		oh						oh	
				she	ba		ba											

dark gray = The one of the song and clave.   light gray = Where the song "punctuates" in the same place as the clave.
Clave or guideline for Finding the 4/4 Groove in the Body (see page on 22)

						Kpanlogo Clave and Song												
Vocables	Ti	Na	Ta	Ke	Ti	Na	Ta	Ke	Ti	Na	Ta	Ke	Ti	Na	Ta	Ke	Ti	Na
Time	3	4	1	2	3	4	1	2	3	4	1	2	3	4	1	2	3	4
Clave					X		X				X			X			X	
Song											oh		she		ba		ba?	oh
				she	ba		ba!											

There is another part of the song in call and response that punctuates in the same place.
I used a question mark and exclamation point to show the call (?) and the response (!).

Sing Three Against Two

Another thing that's great is to learn to sing two rhythmic intervals, such as three and two.

When you combine two different pulses in the same tempo, they make a third musical story. (See Rhythmic Structures, page 16.)

Three Plus Two Make a Song					
1	2	1	2	1	2
1	2	3	1	2	3
go		ba	gu	ba	

2 + 3 subdivision together = go
2 subdivision = ba   3 subdivision = gu

Here comes a more complex three-two song taught to me by Sanga of the Valley. Don't freak out when you see the chart! Remember, you're not doing this alone—it takes a group to sing these songs together! Take one part at a time.

First, notice the "two" interval, called *Ta Ki* or 1 2. Practice using the voice in saying: one two one two one two, etc. Look at the first song and rhythm in the **two** interval. Notice that the song and the rhythm change from the beat to the offbeat—from the one to the two **midway** in the song. This rhythm's song also describes something that happens in many African rhythms: the first note (the *ye*) is also the last note we sing—the snake will bite its own tail. Usually you begin singing the song on the first *Ma*: *Ma-Ma-solo-so-ee-ye*. Just remember that the *ye* is the *one*.

							The Two Interval					
Vocables	*Ta*	*Ki*	*Ta*	*Ki*	*Ta*	*Ki*	*Ta*	*Ki*	*Ta*	*Ki*	*Ta*	*Ki*
Time	1	2	1	2	1	2	1	2	1	2	1	2
Song	ye		ma		ma		so	lo		so		ee
Drum	do		pa		pa		pa	pa		pa		go

This second rhythm group shows you the "three" interval, or *Ga Ma La*. Practice using the voice in saying: one two three, one two three, one two three. Feel the three interval. Most of the syllables that we sing in this song are on the *one*:

Hey - - go - - bum ba di ye - -

	The Three Interval											
Vocables	*Ga*	*Ma*	*La*	*Ga*	*Ma*	*La*	*Ga*	*Ma*	*La*	*Ga*	*Ma*	*La*
Time	1	2	3	1	2	3	1	2	3	1	2	3
Song	hey			go			bum	ba	di	ye		
Drum	Gun	go	do	Gun	go	do	Gun	go	do	Gun	go	do

Notice the difference in the feel of the two intervals. They are like two (2) different characters. The three has more swing, like a waltz. The two reminds me of yes and no—very direct.

	Three Interval Song											
Vocables	*Ga*	*Ma*	*La*	*Ga*	*Ma*	*La*	*Ga*	*Ma*	*La*	*Ga*	*Ma*	*La*
Time	1	2	3	1	2	3	1	2	3	1	2	3
Drum	Gun		go	do	go		Gun		go	do	go	
3 Song	ee		wi	de	tay		ee		wi	de	tay	
Song	ee		wi	de	tay		my				my	

The third rhythm is also in the three feel. *Ga - La Ga Ma -* is the structure of the song with the syllables that follow: *ee – wi de tay -* three times, followed by *my* (first note) - - - *my* (ends on the last note that you play on the drum).

The best way to hear the complexity of this music is to play the drum on the cross pattern and sing the other two vocal accompaniments. This can be a challenging exercise. Try to listen to the other parts as you sing the part you have chosen. Gradually allow the drum to soften its intensity as you continue singing: gradually fade out the drum and you end up with only the voice. You will hear the parts in a completely new way as you sing them—hearing the groove of the three and two.

If you play this in a group orchestration there is an amazing moment when the voices all come together on the *one*—(the sung syllables of *ye*, *hey*, and *ee*). It's like a big wave comes crashing on the shore, then the melodies disperse, and they gather and wham, crash again. This is the rhythm in its entirety!

Put It All Together! Three Against Two, Song and Drum												
2 Interval	Ta	Ki	Ta	Ki	Ta	Ki	Ta	Ki	Ta	Ki	Ta	Ki
Time	1	2	1	2	1	2	1	2	1	2	1	2
Song	ye		ma		ma		so	lo		so		ee
Drum	*do*		*pa*		*pa*		*pa*	*pa*		*pa*		*go*
3 Interval	Ga	Ma	La	Ga	Ma	La	Ga	Ma	La	Ga	Ma	La
Time	1	2	3	1	2	3	1	2	3	1	2	3
Song	hey			go			bum	ba	di	ye		
Drum	*Gun*	*go*	*do*	*Gun*	*go*	*do*	*Gun*	*go*	*do*	*Gun*	*go*	*do*
Drum 3	*Gun*		*go*	*do*	*go*		*Gun*		*go*	*do*	*go*	
3 Song	ee		wi	de	tay		ee		wi	de	tay	
	ee		wi	de	tay		my				my	

Complex Body Games in Four

You need a pair of ankle bells, a shaker, and a clicker for this exercise.

Step *na ta* starting with your left foot and get the shaker going in your right hand for *ti na*. That could take a while. Enjoy the ride.

See video: www.WholePersonDrummingBook.com (Complex Games in Four).

	Complex Body Games in Four								
Vocables	Na	Ta	Ke	Ti	Na	Ta	Ke	Ti	Na
Time	1	2	3	4	1	2	3	4	1
Step	L	R			R	L			
Shaker				▼	▲			▼	▲
1.		click				click			
2.				click				click	
3.		click				click			
4.				click				click	
5.				click	click			click	click

▼ = shaker is on its head
▲ = shaker has its bottom down!

- Once you have established the ability to step on *na ta* and shake your shaker on *ti na*, begin to sing a song that includes all four "notes." See if you can hear the ankle bells and hear the shaker. See if you can form an inner picture of the structure you are creating by stepping and moving your hand.

- Eventually, as you get more comfortable with this pattern, begin to click on the *one* (*Ta*)! As it is the *one* or primary pulse, it will feel very grounding.
- Continue with 2, 3, and 4, returning as often as possible to 1 2 3 4 or *TaKeTiNa*.

In this exercise it is important to **take your time**. Instead of rushing from one element of the exercise to another, feel the landscape with your entire being. As long as you are speaking the syllables, you will be able to stay in the present moment and not get lost with your footsteps and hands. Start over often.

Fall out often.

Have fun!

chapter five

Further Meditations on Learning the Drum

One of our drum circle sites in Palo Alto Baylands

Drum Circles

I spent my early drumming development loving both random and planned drum circles.

I would play anywhere and anytime. It was such a rush. I mentioned earlier that I had an epiphany that sent me on the search to become a better drummer and musician. Still, I loved the sacred and profane gatherings at the Palo Alto Baylands, the Stanford New Guinea Sculpture Garden, our local parks, and various people's houses. The excitement, the possibility of lift-off—of the group actually going somewhere—was so compelling and addictive.

Groove is sexy and steamy, and being "in the pocket" is *It*—the greatest opportunity for a natural high! There is always a potential for that magical connection to occur in drum circles, whether or not it actually happens.

A good facilitator is a gift. If no one was facilitating, anything could happen, and sometimes did.

My students have asked more than once: how do you figure out what to play at a drum circle?

Left: New Guinea Sculpture Garden, Stanford, home of many drum circles

- Start with your pulse. Feel the pulse of the group and find one simple beat that you can clap or step to. Begin by playing that one simple note and just repeating it every so often, until you begin to feel a part of the beat. This can take a little bit of time, so be patient. One note will help you lock into the group pulse.

- Let the one note evolve. If you stay aware, your hands will gradually say something more. People often think they have to do something clever. Instead, just let the music come to you. You may find yourself playing more notes naturally without a lot of forethought. Keep listening to the group.

- Leave space. Allow room for the breath. Disengage briefly from time to time. That means STOP PLAYING now and then. You can listen more deeply to what is going on around you and then re-engage. Reorient yourself the moment you feel confused. Maybe you lost the connection temporarily. Take time to find yourself, so you can lose yourself in the music again.

Although anything is possible at a drum circle, etiquette and inclusion are appreciated!

- Respect the drum and its owner. If you see an "empty" drum in the middle of a circle, it is usually a signal that the instrument is available to be played. Still, it is polite to ask or indicate, "Hey, is this open for grabs?" Then treat it nicely! Return it to the center when you're finished.

- **Take off your rings to play**—especially if you're going to play someone else's drum!

- Try different sound shapers. Bells, rattles, clave sticks, boom whackers all add a great sound to the mix and are as important and vital to the sound of a group as the drum.

- Try to find a way to engage. Make eye contact with others in the circle. Pick a friendly person to sit near, and begin a conversation with your instruments. Or find someone across the circle to connect to. If it isn't fun, don't play. Remember, you are communicating. You have more choices than shouting.

- Put the drum down, get up, and dance! Baba used to say that the moment that you can no longer sit in your chair and you have to move to the music is your healing moment! If you're playing for a ceremony or ritual, it is necessary to play until the event has ended; but in a casual gathering of your peers, get up and shake yourself out. You may inspire the other drummers to play more cohesively just by moving and grooving to the sound around you.

Storytelling and the Healing Power of the Drum

Some of my teachers, especially Baba, Ma Boukaka, and Sanga of the Valley, were gifted storytellers as well as drummers. They could smell when there was too much tension in the room. Then they would tell a story. Some of the stories were deeply moving, about the meaning of a rhythm or a song. Some of the stories were educational—like the story of the creation of the village "police," the meaning of the word "*cult*" within a village society, or how within a village *slavery* was a means of social correction. Stories about roosters that are spokespeople, about snails and how the snail shows that we, too, can be provided for. Stories about the Middle Passage and breaking free from slavery. Stories about how to heal yourself.

Some drummers would be chomping at the bit to get back to drumming; but looking around the room, you could see how these stories would relax the group as a whole. The power of sitting around the fire listening to the elders was brought to life. Time stopped and there we were again in our tribal village.

Akiwowo, Baba's cousin, told me once that some musical rhythms came from the rhythmic nature of work. He also said drummers could listen to sounds of nature—the calling of birds from one place to another or the sounds of tree frogs or insects, and mimic those sounds in drum music. My teachers also explained the meaning of pouring libation (looks like pouring liquid on the ground), or picking certain herbs at certain times of day. All of the stories opened a sense of wonder about the natural world, and of a pre-modern world filled with meaning and magic. And all these stories added to the power of drumming as a means of social connection, healing, and passing on a legacy.

I began to feel that rhythms could be seen as medicine for the soul. That is, in a certain situation playing a certain rhythm would encourage our spirits to move in a particular way. This made sense not only in what we chose to play but also in *how we intended to play*.

Yaya Diallo in his book, *The Healing Drum*, speaks about diagnosing and curing mental illness through the drum. Baba talked about the healing power of the drum. Through the stories of indigenous healing, I felt that despite what we Euro-Americans know about medicine, we don't know as much about healing.

My dear friend Samba Ngo, an extraordinary musical artist, told me stories about his father, who was an *nganga*, or healer. His father would use the *nsambi or nkisi*, a two-string musical instrument made of wood and palm fiber, for diagnosing his clients and finding out the right herb for healing. Samba also said his father specialized in those with sickness in the mind. For that kind of sickness, a healing ceremony would be necessary.

The hardest thing for Western untrained drummers is playing something completely simple over and over and over again. Yet it seems that simplicity and repetition are some of the components necessary for healing sickness in the mind. The seeming monotony of the music gives the mind an opportunity to rest. As the monotony and boredom sets in, the mental oppression and depression have a chance to become unstuck—as if the music clears out the unwanted mental chatter.

Seem far-fetched? What do medical intuitives do? The use of drums and music to aid the shaman to step into an altered state has been reported for many years. Still, it is fascinating to our limited Western minds, which are both tantalized and wary of these ideas. We call it magical thinking! I call it the resonating power of rhythm and music to invite healing.

Visualization for Chi Drumming

I feel it is important to be a mindful drummer (and human). I have learned various ways to stay focused while I drum. One method is using guided visualization in my playing. In this chapter I combine visualization with what I call *Chi drumming* to talk about the energy that we can initiate and augment while playing our drums. You can try this exercise and see if it works for you.

Chi Drumming Exercise

Listen to your breathing for a few moments.

Speak with your rhythmic voice what you intend to play on the drum. There are two easy patterns on the following page, or perhaps you have one of your own. Try something simple and easily repeated. This will allow you to tune your energy inward while you play.

Start to play the drum slowly, connecting the sounds with your rhythmic voice. (*Gun, go do, pa ta*)

Bring your attention to your breathing.

Allow a relationship to develop between your breath and your playing—consistent patterns of breathing concurrent with rhythmic phrases.

For example:

Hands move, let's say, in the **Cross pattern**, or the **4 Flow pattern**, in an alternating pattern that is easy to let go of and let happen.

4 Flow Pattern															
Ta	Ke	Ti	Na	Ta	Ke	Ti	Na	Ta	Ke	Ti	Na	Ta	Ke	Ti	Na
1	2	3	4	1	2	3	4	1	2	3	4	1	2	3	4
R	L	R	L	R	L	R	L	R	L	R	L	R	L	R	L
Gun	Gun	go	do	Gun	Gun	go	do	Gun	Gun	go	do	Gun	Gun	go	do

OR

Cross Pattern											
Ga	Ma	La	Ga	Ma	La	Ga	Ma	La	Ga	Ma	La
1	2	3	1	2	3	1	2	3	1	2	3
R	L	R	L	R	L	R	L	R	L	R	L
Gun	do	go	Gun	go	do	Gun	do	go	Gun	go	do

See if your breathing can become a part of what you're doing while you drum. Be aware of how you breathe (inhale and exhale) while drumming.

Feel the pattern. Keep to the pattern. Synchronize and ground. Attend to what you are doing.

See how much of your body you can feel as you play; loosen the belly, let the shoulder blades slide down and support the back, loosen the jaw, lips and tongue. Feel the backs of your thighs pressing down in the seat, if you're sitting, your spine pulling upward. Feel yourself poised more on the edge of your seat than sitting back, allowing energy in your legs. If you're sitting, imagine that you have a big, broad, alligator or kangaroo tail (also mentioned on page 14) that you can lean into.

If you're standing, try to feel a neutral stance with your pelvis. Soften all the gateways—the ankles, the knees, and the thighs. Soften your hips as you stand and drum.

Continue drumming, at a tempo that you can easily keep up for a period of time.

At a certain point, begin to bring your awareness into the area right below your belly button, and slightly back toward the spinal column. Can you find that place with your awareness? It is called *dan tien* in Eastern meditation and martial art practices. It helps to keep your belly very relaxed.

This is a worthwhile practice. Developing *chi* drumming involves feeling the endpoints of where you think you can drum now—and then, with respect, being willing to lose that limitation.

Each time you come to the drum, it will be different. But you have to be the one to start to develop this strength and focus. When you do, you will not have to play loud in order to be heard.

Play consciously for five minutes, at least three times per week.

Keep yourself alert whenever you are practicing—either working on technique, flow, or leading with your non-dominant side.

Practice ten minutes of <u>stamina drumming</u> one day a week.

(See exercises in How to Practice With the Drum, page 27, as well as in Increase Your Speed and Stamina, page 55.)

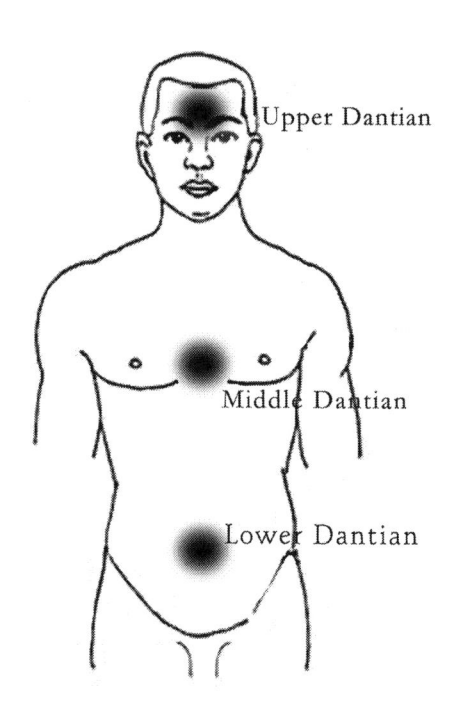

Play the Parts that Support the Rhythm

Go to a drum circle or jam where there is a blend of drummers, some with experience, some new to the game. How many of them are willing to play the same rhythm for more than five minutes? Those are the ones I want in my band!

When I went to Africa the first time, I studied at the Center for African Music and Dance in Legon, Accra, Ghana. Dr. J. H. Kwabena Nketia, one of the first African ethnomusicologists, founded the center for preserving the music and dance of Ghana. I spoke to him for a newsletter I was publishing at the time—*Village Heartbeat*.

My question to Dr. Nketia was: If you had any message to give to Western (i.e. American and European) drummers, what would it be?

His answer was simple: Play the parts that support the rhythm.

Most of us like change. You might think that if you are playing one simple part for an extended period of time your part will be boring, and you've got to do something to spice it up. Don't.

Staying with a rhythm for an extended period of time *expands* all the following:

a) **Your understanding of the music that you're playing**

   Somehow when you settle into a groove with one part, you begin to hear the other parts in relation to it. That's how to understand and replicate drum orchestration. It's like listening to crickets on a summer's eve. In time, you can hear how the parts interlock, call, and respond to one another.

b) **Your ability to hold onto rhythm**

   It is like being in meditation. Meditation is not all peaceful and quiet. It is an opportunity to drop into one place and watch all the chaos that is swirling around inside you and every one of us. You get to see your thoughts—how you drift away, and when you do, what happens to the rhythm. Are you even in the room with the drum? Come back and note how interestingly complex it is to hold onto one rhythm. What stops us from being here now?

c) **Your ability to serve the rhythm**

   Play that one rhythm as if it is the most important thing that you could ever do in your life! What a great attitude! If you see that your part is necessary and important to the music, you will be less likely to be distracted, and your playing will feed the group and yourself.

I love the top parts in orchestrations. I love the stuff with the slaps and tones and fancy handwork. BUT, and here's the big BUT—if no one is holding down the basic orchestration, *there is no music*.

The bottom rules, the bottom grooves. The bottom holds the container of the rhythm. I get drunk and heady with playing the top parts from time to time. But I play that bottom, because I can sound just as good on a bottom part as I sound on the top.

In the *TaKeTiNa* rhythm process, the leader doesn't add complexity in the call and response until almost everyone feels their feet securely grounded in the basic rhythm. No matter how often we might disturb the rhythm by adding some interesting riff, we return repeatedly to the familiar to ground ourselves. Returning to home base is how stability in music is built. Allow small fluctuations into the unknown and return to grounding the bottom.

Improvisation comes from a deep understanding of the rhythm that you are playing. When we understand a drum pattern we can leave out notes or add notes while playing. I would call that *improvisation within the family of rhythms*. Finally, as the rhythm is more and more internalized, you begin to take little forays into outer space, at the same time as hearing the rhythm continuing in the background.

Similarly, in a drum circle when one part of the circle is sculpted out and continues to play, the facilitator can bring different accents into your playing while you experience the groove going on in the background!

Enjoy the part that you play in your group!

Competition

When I first began to drum with Baba, I had a vision for community. It emerged from the impassioned feeling of wholeness and spirit that I experienced when I drummed in his classes. (I imagined others felt that way too.) Along with Baba's stories, and stories passed on by my other teachers, I imagined we could be an enlightened community. I projected my greatest hopes and wishes for us to be like one big, loving tribe, with each person recognized for the gifts and talents that they bring to the table. I don't think I ever got over the sixties and the picture of unity that those times offered.

Our culture is not so perfect. I thought non-white, earth-based cultures seemed to have more soul. My hope and projection was that these other cultures might be more humane, grounded, more based on wisdom than greed—with less competition and social hierarchy.

So here we are, on drums, right? Tame little instruments. We are going to share about love, peace, healing, and joy while drumming. Wrong. At least my entry into this world was nothing like that.

When I entered drumming there was one female drummer for each seven males. In the beginning, I loved the odds. I mean, surrounded with male energy, WOW! I thought I would be supported and protected by my drum brothers.

What fantasy movie did I drop into? Sadly, it wasn't like that. Instead, I fell into a world of competition like I had never experienced before.

Given that little piece of a story, I will cut to the chase and say this: Competition and comparison do not work with drumming, or anything else, really. But especially drumming.

Signs of competition in a drum group

- Lack of eye contact or bodily acknowledgement of your presence
- Increasing volume
- Increasing speed
- The "stink-eye," turning body away
- Tension and lack of breath in the music and the room

How to tame your own competitive nature in a drum group

In order to use drumming as a path to wholeness, you have to arrive. Be here now with your hands on the drum and your spine straight and feet firmly planted on the ground. Begin to listen to yourself. Is there self-commentary regarding what you are playing? Inner criticism or self-consciousness? Confusion? "What do I play with this beat?"

Check for tension in your body-mind. Is there excitement or fear? As you listen to yourself, take time to tune yourself to the music occurring in the room, or introduce a <u>simple</u> beat.

After you have arrived in the room with others, take one other person in the room into your awareness. If you cannot hear them, see if you can quiet down enough to make what they are playing audible to you. If you cannot hear them, watch their hands. See if you can synchronize with their movements. When you become aware of one other person, a shift will occur.

Try this again with another drummer. As you continue to do this with random people in the circle, you will begin to feel more connected to the whole.

Some ways to encourage cooperative drumming

- Open eyes: Allow the room and the people in it to come into your vision. It's a good idea not to look directly at anyone; even dogs think that's aggressive. Begin to use more peripheral vision.

- Open face: Keep looking outward into the room. See what's happening. Any dancers? What are the kids doing? Who is drumming with eyes closed?

- Open *affect* (the mood or emotion you express): when the rhythm starts to rock, enjoy it, and show that you hear the music. See if you can make one connection with another person in a mild way—nodding, smiling, playing toward each other.

- Sit back and let the rhythm cook.

- If the rhythm has a form, you can put a lid on it—or contain it. Contain the music through maintaining the rhythm speed and adding heat. The heat comes from your attention and presence while you drum. (See Visualization for Chi Drumming, page 86). So presence + consistency = lift off!

Even if your tribe is in the "loud is better" stage of drum community, you can begin to shape the tendency of the drum group by *serving the rhythm*. This is one of those times when it is not all about me and what I can do, but playing in the background. The real artistry of drumming together is knowing when it is appropriate to goose the group, *and* knowing when you have the skills to make that happen. If you don't have the skills yet, then serve the rhythm by playing one easy part with heart and feeling.

Sleeping and Rhythm

There are things that we learn musically and rhythmically with our waking consciousness—movements of our hands and/or feet. We can attend to our body position, recall rhythmic parts, see notes written in unit box notation, and learn by counting or by feeling the spaces in drum patterns or rhythm figures.

Another kind of learning happens when we sleep or rest. It has nothing to do with what we are trying to acquire, grasp or pursue mentally. It is the dots that connect us from being in rhythm to staying in rhythm. It is how rhythm guides us and informs us.

How does this happen? I have a theory.

When we stay in the field of music and movement for a period of time, a resonance lingers long after the music stops. This resonance, or perhaps some rhythmic patterns, continues to play in our minds, bodies, and souls. This lingering sound memory stimulates and feeds the intuitive, spatial, nonverbal part of the brain.

We have heard stories of scientists discovering amazing things that come to them from dream states, and Albert Einstein stated in no uncertain terms that the theory of relativity was a "musical thought" that came to him intuitively. Einstein said: "If I were not a physicist, I would probably be a musician. I often think in music. I live my daydreams in music."

The intuitive sense of time and space is not interrupted by the thinking mind during sleep, meditation, and deep relaxation.

When we try too hard to get it, there is rigidity or spasticity in our movements. When we sleep or relax our bodies can re-create those movements in a smooth, uninterrupted way.

The next time we encounter the same exercise or set of movements, our bodies remember that sense of spaciousness that occurred in sleep. The next attempt is less harried, more fluid. I call this intuitive learning—even though we did nothing to make it happen!

When working with stroke victims, Feldenkrais Method practitioners (a type of bodywork) invite the client simply to remember, to imagine or visualize, movements that the body cannot produce voluntarily. By doing so, they find that new neural pathways develop to recreate the original movement. This neuroplasticity means that we are constantly learning, when given the right stimuli.

And in my own experience, when I'm trying to understand an unusual rhythmic structure with my whole body, my performance improves after I sleep on it.

This is one of the most important reasons for trainings or workshops that include several days in a row of intense learning. Sleeping in between the daily lessons supports the active learning during the day.

Solar and Lunar Drumming

The symbolism of the sun is strongly present in our world today. The sun is fiery and far-reaching, but oblivious of all it consumes. Feeding on itself, it always threatens to die from overconsumption. It shows its worst in the mechanics of a society fixated on making, having, and acquiring.

And yet each day we wake to the magnificence of living in the world of light and color, where we see shape and form, and all appears to us in its beauty. Without the sun, we would not exist for long. Our sources of food and nourishment would disappear. Where would we be without the light of day to give us hope?

In contrast, the symbolic message of the moon tells us of a being that reflects light but does not generate its own. The moon is an example of receptivity, a great power of becoming. As we know, the moon governs the tides in the oceans and shows us the possibility of experiencing a cycle with darkness waning, light waxing to fullness, and then waning back again to dark.

In the dark is mystery—things seem to manifest out of the void.

The moon symbolizes for us the ability to be reflective, listening, receptive, and flowing. The moon allows us to rest, to dream, in the softened images of the night. The moon invites us to turn our attention to the lunar qualities of our being: allowing, not knowing, patience.

Losing one's way, experiencing a lack of purpose or initiative, is the downside to being moonstruck. The path becomes hidden or fraught with obstacles that seem overwhelming in the darkness.

In the world of music and specifically drumming and percussion, we can clearly hear and see the effects of solar drumming. The excited passion and the fiery chops that come from traditions of African drumming, the core strength in Taiko drumming, the long continuous grooves in a drum circle—all can have the hot quality of the sun. We need strength to play for long periods of time, but more than strength and stamina, we have to have a kind of brightness, a willing, happy energy to persevere in our playing, through thick and thin, through all the boredom that comes from continuity of movement, passing through judging the people we're playing with or the music. This brightness could be called a sunny joy; it comes through the control of the breath. By controlling the breath, we can ride the heat, not be burnt by it. The difference lies in feeling a warmth that invigorates rather than a heat that exhausts.

Undeveloped solar drumming is personified in a man or woman who takes over, playing the loudest or the fastest. They might be highly talented and yet show untrained sun-ness, undeveloped creativity. Trained solar drumming is inclusive. Through our warmth, we inspire and strengthen everyone else in a circle, class, or band. We encourage us all to build the big house of rhythm together and invite everyone inside.

Every day must have its night.

Lunar drumming at its best is noticing the intervals between the notes. The focus turns toward *listening* as much as doing, and feeling *what* is the right event or instrument to add to the mix. It might be a wind chime or rainstick. Or a voice that soars with the other instruments.

The opposite of the joy of worshipping the interval and all the potential music within, is getting lost, lost, lost in the void—losing the *one*—losing the sense of where the beat begins and ends in a cycle.

"Mooniness" is accompanied by a lack of energy. The rhythm lacks starch, focus. Undeveloped lunar drumming could be seen in a group where no one has the energy or stamina, confidence or knowledge, to coax the groove into consistent repetition. Is it a group fear of making mistakes? Or is it people who don't know how to self-organize or allow themselves to lead?

To be sure, we need all of it—the sun and the moon, the heat and the coolness.

Can we recognize what is needed when we play together?

Perhaps the greatest challenge is to listen outside of ourselves. Do we turn up the heat by playing the bottom with energy and joy to show a solid rhythm foundation? Or tune in more intently to what is being "said" and adding the simplest of sounds at the right moment? To actively listen in this way will bring a renewed sense of connectedness and wholeness to the music. A group of musicians working to fine-tune themselves will not only produce a more interesting and groovy sound, it will be a group of people on a path of self-discovery and growth.

Building the Container—Holding On With Your Heart

You might remember that I am a drum circle snob. After my breakthrough experience of realizing that loud sound was not necessarily music, I became much more attached to intentionally creating music. However, I am also well aware of the positive effect of just touching a drum. I see the joy and excitement it produces in people—just to make a simple sound.

There is a definite and wonderful place for the community drum circle. Leaderless, it can be a quiet, meditative experience with frame drums, or a loud, sprawling, thunder-drumming free-for-all taking no prisoners nohow!

Facilitated drum circles can give participants a chance to play a variety of instruments or hear a variety of voices—to begin to see or hear how different instruments shape the music and are sometimes in the background because of the loudness of the drum. Drum circles that are facilitated can deal with special populations: youth-at-risk, mentally different, children with learning disabilities, people with Alzheimer's, autism, corporate isolation—you name it.

For example, Heather MacTavish, who was diagnosed with Parkinson's disease in 1995, created methods for using rhythm and drums to work with people with chronic, degenerative, and developmental disabilities, which she refers to as *extraordinary* abilities. Heather's gatherings look more like a sing-along than the kind of drum circle you might see on the beach in Santa Barbara, but the principle of creating community and healing through music is the same. She uses singing old-time songs with a simple heartbeat drum pulse to connect people to their musical memories.

A recent video called "Alive Inside" shows the connection between music and memory, and how parts of the brain that have retained musical memory can connect us to the present world. Music and pulsation is *that* close to our human experience.

A quantum leap can happen when a drumming circle's music changes from random pulsation to coherent information—"lift off"—cohesive sound! We begin to synchronize, or as Micky Hart calls it in his book, *Drumming on the Edge of Magic*, we *entrain*. We are no longer having to THINK about joining others in playing. The entire field has dropped into playing together. Those are magical moments.

Until that happens, we can play rhythms together with intent and heart. Here is an exercise that can help in building a container for the music to cook in!

Play one of these two rhythms intentionally, for a long time. A great example of how to do this is Baba's rhythmic patterns numbers 1 and 3.

Baba's Rhythmic Patterns Numbers 1 and 3.												
Vocables	Ga	Ma	La	Ga	Ma	La	Ga	Ma	La	Ga	Ma	La
Time	1	2	3	1	2	3	1	2	3	1	2	3
Pattern 1	Gun		go	do			Gun		go	do		
Pattern 3	Gun		go	do	go	do	Gun		go	do		

This is easy to play for a while! And play this rhythm with it: the cross pattern.

The Cross Pattern												
Vocables	Ga	Ma	La	Ga	Ma	La	Ga	Ma	La	Ga	Ma	La
Time	1	2	3	1	2	3	1	2	3	1	2	3
Drum	Gun	go	do	Gun	go	do	Gun	go	do	Gun	go	do

Here is the trick: *you must play with intent.* Playing with intent means being here, now. (Playing with intent does not mean playing louder.) Any rhythm is just a rhythm until you apply intention and attention. Even the simplest of orchestrations can take off and fly if you stick with what you are playing until real heat gets generated.

Then you can add this third easy accompaniment (which I am noting in rhythmic language):

Accompaniment/Top Rhythm												
Ga	Ma	La	Ga	Ma	La	Ga	Ma	La	Ga	Ma	La
1	2	3	1	2	3	1	2	3	1	2	3
go		pa	ta			go		pa	ta		
go		pa	ta	pa	ta	go		pa	ta		

Since this is melodically a higher pitched timbre on the drum, it can act as the "top" rhythm. When you enter the rhythm in the right place, with the right energy (all of which is vague in writing), you can rock the room with this super simple groove.

Clue: Do not play the top until the bottom begins to cook!

Think about that word, "cook." Think about when food starts to cook in your kitchen…you can smell it! Hopefully it smells good! Rhythm is the same way. You can't begin to put toppings on something until the rhythm is really warm through and through. BE PATIENT. If you set something on the heat and stir it every once in a while, it will cook. You can also put a lid on the pot and it will build more energy. That is the *intent* part of playing. You can't get lost in your dream world. Stay with the rhythm. If you get bored, put more attention into what you are playing: say the notes, sit up straight, or whatever helps you to stay grounded. And enjoy the process.

Personally, I get this feeling of heat in my body, especially in my solar plexus on down to my gut. When it's a perfect container (and it can be), you will know the right moment to play the top part. Actually, you couldn't stop yourself if you tried! The top energizes, adds more fuel to the fire. It may take some time to get there, but all of it, all of it, should be exciting and energizing. Just like warm-ups before you really lift off into the ecstasy of dancing.

By the way, this is still different from soloing. A solo is like rapping. It is your own expression, within the rules of rhythm—tempo and subdivision. In order to solo you need to internally understand how much space you have to rap in. And you also have to know, feel, sense, the tempo of the rhythm.

You really have to get some heat up for launching off into a solo. Heat rises—like the solo can rise above the melody. Most importantly, when you solo you want to make sure that the whole house of rhythm cards doesn't collapse. If you haven't baked the souffle enough it won't stay up and puffy!

I am a good beginning drum teacher and I can tell you that you don't have to be at a virtuoso level of skill to get to this kind of wonderful state of playing bottom, middle accompaniments, or the top. You just have to be willing to a) focus and b) keep playing.

Think of the rhythm like a ritual and the solo like the prayer. So you think you have never been in a ritual? Yes, you have. A great athletic event or a powerful concert can have the same effect.

Build the container (create the event, invite the people, buy the tickets), cook the food (bring your energy into it, commit to the moment, engage in the process), and finally begin to let go. Say your prayer or talk to the you that you love, or connect to the amazing quality of nature—anything that leaves the little self behind and connects you to a sense of bigger awareness and presence. You will recognize the right moment to let go into the top part, I assure you. It is that moment that is so exciting and powerful, happy and fulfilling, connected, grounded, and spiritual all at once. You will feel like singing. You will feel like dancing.

Don't. Stay with the drum. Your job is to be the container, the builder of fiery energy—the holder of the rhythm. There will be a moment when the circle begins to tire and the energy is winding down. Before it all falls apart, call the break!

Whew!

Now close your eyes. Go within. Feel with your whole body, from the tips of your toes to the hair on your head.

Don't trivialize the moment. This is what we are here on the planet for.

The Art of Mastery

Mastery, as George Leonard describes it in his book with that name, runs counter to the American goal-oriented ethic. Mastery is a process, not a product. You never actually get there, wherever "there" is. Or you might see it differently: you are always there and there's no place to get.

This book has been an exercise in mastery for me. As soon as I started thinking about it, I wanted to be done. I wanted the fully realized, finished product, proof of my mastery, to exist, right then. Right now!

My head was filled with thoughts and questions. How many pages are enough? Is this a stupid idea? Who will buy it? Does it have value? Does it have to have a DVD with it? Because if it does, that means a lot more work, and oh boy, I am getting tired already.

Oh no, I didn't write anything today. Boy, that was a brilliant idea. I wonder if anyone will like this? Am I a good writer? Who is going to edit this for me? Oh my god, they are going to see the messiness of my mental closet! I am never going to be finished! Am I done yet? Am I cooked yet?

But *Mastery* says it is the journey that shapes our lives, not arriving at one final point. Man, I hate that. I want the gold star and to be written up in *Who's Who*, *Wikipedia* and *People* magazine too. Now. Not later. NOW!

I know better. The things that draw me—the things to which I have dedicated my life—drumming, rhythm meditations, journaling, gardening, art, yoga, dance—none of these things are about a finite point of arrival. I've learned that. Every time I teach one of my classes in drumming, I have another opportunity to check my technique, see how my body feels, all in the moment. I am focusing, breathing, relaxing, noting, noting, noting, doing what I teach and encourage my students to do. I am part of the rhythm, part of everything around me, part of the music. It is HAPPENING.

The sense of being on the journey breaks down afterwards. After an event I make plans for the next moment or want to judge what occurred. It is hard to let oneself travel on a journey without knowing the final outcome. But that is also what traveling is about! Leaving the known, going into the new, and returning again to what we know but with new eyes and a fresh perspective.

When I am reading a really good book—one that is suspenseful and engaging—when the tension builds I feel a growing compulsion to skip to the end and learn the book's destination. On a life path I experience that same tension, but I don't get to jump to the end of my life to relieve my questioning mind. All I can do is imagine the ending. But that reveals the difference between books and life. In life we never know how things end because we never get there. All we can know—all I can know—is what's in the moment.

It is hard for me to accept living with the unknown. And yet it is the easiest thing to do; the simplest place to be; the only place anyone can be. Why would I want to be any place other than the perfect now? Still I do. I am I in the past and then off to an imagined future.

I have learned to develop practices—walking, yoga, writing, meditating, and drumming that help me stay engaged in the here and now.

I tell myself and I teach my students: if you focus, you can see yourself—in the moments you play, or the moments you engage in those other practices. From time to time, I tell them, and myself, we are lucky or blessed enough to experience a kind of resonance—a hint of what traveling on the path of mastery gives us.

And then, I tell myself and my students: we begin again.

	Your Own Expression, Within the Rules of Rhythm
1	2	3	4	1	2	3	4
Yo	ur	so	ng	is	this	lo	ong
1 2	3 4	1 2	3 4	1 2	3 4	1 2	3 4
you	can	al so	div	ide	it	like	this
1234	1234	1234	1234	1234	1234	1234	1234
oooo	oooo	oooo	ooor	this	oooo	oooo	oooo
1	2	3	1	2	3	1	2
You	Can	HAVE	A	group	Like	this	YES
BUUUT	THE	SPPPACE	IIIIISSS	SSTTTILLL	THIIISS	LOOO	OONNG

Interviews

An Interview with Alalade Frederick

Source: *Village Heartbeat* Vol. 2, No. 4, September 1994

Alalade is the dance captain for Babatunde Olatunji's Drums of Passion troupe. Alalade's understanding of the body and "working the earth" makes her a unique teacher. She is able to break down the subtlety of African dance movements for even non-dancers to understand. She has a dance company called Ojoba (Day of New Creations).

VHB: *As a dancer and performer, what do you see as the relationship, both real and ideal, between the drummer and the dancer?*

A: I am a family person and we have a family company. Our focus is to generate that connection between the dance and the drum, because you're telling a story, actually a way of telling history.

If you don't have the music to carry you through, what it is you are trying to tell with the movement doesn't happen; you can't feel that. Because it is a partnership, a relationship, so if you separate them, you don't get the fullness of what you are trying to say. It's only half of it. It's a connection, a relationship.

It pulls over into your "real" life in how you deal with your family, your children, your friends and relatives. Being able to listen, being able to communicate, to be flexible and trying to compromise, trying to find a way of being able to do what you want to do and express yourself, but also let the other person be what they want and express themselves, and in the same space.

VHB: *Do you have any examples or stories to share of how it was for you when you were in the process of learning to work with drummers?*

A: There are times when it doesn't seem to be happening. You can't feel the dance, you can't feel the rhythm. Drummers will drum and they'll get into themselves, they're into the music, and the dancer might be dancing for herself. They never learned how to talk to each other. They weren't taught that. That is something that the Africans do naturally because they've lived it, but we in America, drummers were taught separately: "These are the drum rhythms, this is how you get into that." Dancers were taught, "These are the movements, you gotta do this." But they were never taught, "You've got to listen to the drum. If he says this, you should be responding this way." It's actually a communication thing happening.

Before I met my husband, I had been dancing three years in African dance and only working with drummers in classes. I wanted to start a program in the Bronx, because we didn't have anything happening in the Bronx culturally. Everything was happening in either Brooklyn or Manhattan.

But I didn't have any funds. I wanted to try something, an experiment, but I needed a drummer, and I had no money to pay a drummer. I needed someone who would be willing to work with me.

I met my husband in a dance class that I was teaching at City College, and he had very good energy. He had studied to be a priest, had just come out of his initiation process, and I said to him, "I'm going to do this thing in the Bronx. Would you mind working with me, and there's no money, but blah, blah, blah." You know, the whole nine yards. He said, "Sure, I'd love to do that with you." It was something he wanted to do also.

But when we started working together…He comes from a family that actually dances. His mother has a dance school, so he was into dancing as well as the drum. I was not used to relating to the drummer. We were having problems. He would say, "You're not listening to the rhythm." I'd say, "Yes, I am, but you're not playing what I'm doing." And what it was is that drum rhythms for dances have phrasing that you can't count 1-2-3-4-5-6-7-8.

You have to do a whole phrasing of the music in order to actually deal with the drum itself, but I didn't know that. My first training was ballet, and I was taught through Dunham and Graham technique to count. In the African arts, you can make the counting work if you know the phrasing. When I learned that, it enabled me to, like Baba said, dance to the beat of the drum. We had not been doing that. We were making our own movement fit whatever we wanted to do.

So in working with this drummer, and he became my mate as well, we had another kind of intimacy going. We were able to leave the dance studio and come home and in the privacy of our own space he'd say, "Well, baby, I know you think this was happening, but this is really what was going on." And I was able to listen, without being all uptight, and start to relate to what was going on. It made the dancing much different than what I conceived it to be. So that's the connection that I see between dancing and the drum.

VHB: *Since African and ethnic dance seems to be more popular, and some of the people coming to classes may be new to this kind of expression, what advice could you give people who are entering into this?*

A: I would say, especially for the African dance, go into it open-minded. Whatever you get out of it, take that.

But be very experimental. Go to different realms, because everyone is not teaching for the same reason, and everybody isn't teaching the same thing.

You can go to some classes and get movement, you get to work your body. In some classes you get a little knowledge about why you are doing what you are doing, in other classes you get the spirituality. The dance and drum mean different things to different people. The only way you can know what you are looking for is to experience differences. You can't get stuck on one realm.

You might say, "well, I study with Alma, and Alma says this is the way you do things." And then you go into another class with Alma's teaching. Someone else is presenting something in another way, and we're so closed because we're already conditioned in one way.

I believe that people should be diverse. They should experience not just Nigeria, or Ghana or Senegal or Congolese, but all areas and from different teachers, because we all have something different to offer. You have to be open, really open, to what it is you are going to receive in African dance, because it is presented in different ways for different reasons.

VHB: *What are some of your feelings and thoughts on the spiritual expression in African dance?*

A: To me, that's the most important for us. We want to put it on a production level, on a stage, but only to get a message to people that would not normally get the message otherwise. It's a culture, a way of life. It's not just something to go out and party, but it enhances your life and being. It revitalizes you and heals you. But in order to get people to think of that, you have to tantalize them, entertain them, to put it on the stage. But just because you put it on the stage, you don't want to lose sight of what message you are really trying to get across.

Yes you put on the costumes, you want the excitement, but you also want the message, the teachings to come through. My husband and I were talking about the rap thing that's going on and Snoop Doggy Dog and the message he's trying to get across. How the youth are receiving it, he's not getting the right thought across. So sometimes we can do things and lose sight of the message. So we should not forget about the spirit of the drum and dance, and what it means in terms of the family and the healing connection. Some of us are getting lost in it.

You can shake, you can drum, we can jam, and forget the full essence of what it's supposed to be. So I really believe in the spiritual aspects of it. I believe in the culture that comes along with it, and it is your responsibility.

When you say you are going to learn African drum and dance, you are not just learning drum and dance. You have a responsibility to learn a lot more—what it represents—how you use it, what you use it for.

Everything is not just for the stage, everything is not just for jamming. Some things are sacred.

VHB: *So much of the teaching seems to be oral, from one drummer to another, or one dancer to another, to find the deeper meaning of what we wear, what the dances and rhythms mean.*
A: We've been spoiled by the way we live and the things that are accessible to us. We can get anything we want. It's sometimes about a dollar. Sometimes we put things on but we don't know what they represent or why we wear them. We're drawn to it for some reason and we take it on.

And a lot of times people won't challenge you. They say, "They don't know what they have on," and that's it.

If you open some of the doors and take down the myths, people are more able to identify with things you are talking about instead of feeling as if things are so foreign to them. Give people the history of who you are and what you're about, stop feeling threatened, like I've got to lock everything up and be secretive. When you give knowledge to a person, it also enlightens you because it's growth for you as well. Everything is not a secret.

We think we hold the key, the only key, but in many other cultures the same customs are prevalent. So when people ask questions about things and are interested, it's for a reason.

We're not into this color thing. One of the things I love about Baba is that he is really into connecting with people. Whether you're black, white, Chinese, brown, if you are akin to my spirit, then that's what I am dealing with. People who can relate do, those who can't don't.

VHB: *What has been your greatest challenge as an African-American woman in the performing arts?*
A: Trying to get people to recognize African cultural dance as they recognize ballet, jazz, and the other arts. See, people still view African cultural dance as not really worthy of the arts label. They think it's a backrooted something, with no foundation, no structure. That it's not really worthy of the acknowledgment it should be given. And this is true in terms of payment as well.

VHB: *Or funding.*
A. That's the main thing. Everybody wants it, but they feel we should give it all for nothing.

I'm not just speaking of major producers, I'm talking about even our own people. We've written contracts to do several weddings. One woman called us last night, recommended by a good friend, and said she was getting married next weekend. She knew it was late, but she wanted to do this with us, and she didn't have much money, but she had really high expectations for what she wanted. WOW, for somebody who doesn't have any money, you're asking a lot. And then when I tried to explain to her, she was indignant. Look at what you're asking for. First you want us to lead the groom in with a processional, then you want us to pour libation, then you want a 45 minute to an hour performance, and you want five dancers, three drummers, and for us to come up to Connecticut takes us out of the city, which means transportation, and you want to give us $300. You wouldn't think twice about spending $2000 for a gown you would wear one day and put it in the closet, 'cause it's gonna be there. It's your value system—what's valuable to you.

We don't get the value that is due as we should, that's the hardest thing. We try to give the culture, literally give it away because a lot of people can't afford certain things. We want to perpetuate it. We want people to see what it's about and where we're rooted. But even in giving it away, people still want you to give more.

We have a class and we say can you all pay a dollar each to help pay for the drummers—and people feel like that's too much. But they'll go downtown to Alvin Ailey, pay $15-20 for a class for an hour and get nothing from it. You get 100 people on the floor, you get stretched out for an hour, and you go home. So that to me is the biggest thing, getting recognition of the value of what our culture is really about.

VHB: *Does the gender aspect of it figure in? Is there sexual politics as well, or is it artists across the board, male and female?*
A: In the cultural realm of African art, for me, it's the artists across the board. In the African arts, women have a big part in that. They don't get played down, because they are needed. They are the ones who largely teach the dancing.

At this dance studio downtown, you have the African brothers teaching the dance, but people still would prefer a woman. The men can give the strength and all that, but they can't give the feminine part of what they are trying to express. And people feel very comfortable with the class as taught by a woman.

The woman in the African realm of dance gets a lot of play. Also, she's a mother, and she's a teacher and a griot, preserving the history of the dance. You'll see more of the women…wearing the traditional clothing. We have to keep that going.

Because we are the teachers and preservers of the culture, we have to play many roles. So we have a lot more visibility.

VHB: *Well, that's great. Is there any final thing you'd like to share before we end this interview?*
A: We all are here on the planet for a reason. We all have a mission, and sometimes the Creator gives more than one person the same job to do.

One person can't do it all. He gives us different avenues to travel to reach those means.

We have to stop as a people, I'm saying, as a black race of people right this second, being threatened by one another by what we have to do and what we have to offer. We're not producing the way we should because we're so busy fighting each other. We're so afraid of "you're in the limelight, you got the name, and if I let you into my circle, you're going to take over." Everybody has a shine, and we need to find our glow and work it.

If I know that Zorina is an excellent organizer and that's not my realm, I'm going to call on her expertise and pay for that. I'm going to call this person because he's an excellent musician. We need to do this more than hold each other back out of fear and envy.

I find we can't get our message across because we're so busy fighting each other, staying on the little top that we're on. And there is room for everybody. That's a struggle for us as a people. Respect is what we're trying to teach the child. We want, we want, we want, but we don't give the same thing back.

An Interview with Arthur Hull
Source: *Village Heartbeat*, Vol. 1, No. 3, September 1993

This interview was written in 1993. Arthur Hull no longer makes drums, but his logo lives on! (His drum design was sold to Remo®.)

Arthur Hull is probably the funniest drummer you'll meet. Whether you're playing one of his ashikos (with the distinctive 4-way arrow in the center), watching him conduct drummers like Leonard Bernstein, or listening to his off-the-wall answering machine messages, you'll never quite see the world in the same mundane way.

VHB: *What drew you to this path?*
AH: My mother's heartbeat. While I was in the womb. It was not a choice. It was like a priest's call to God. If you're a priest, you know it somewhere along the line. You can try to deny it, but your spirituality will always come back. I was called.

VHB: *To what do you attribute the current popularity of the drumming movement?*

AH: I'm in the unique position to see this through many different windows. Little groups—men's groups, women's groups, shaman study groups, ethnic arts groups representing their culture through drumming, music and voice, and not least the-hippie-thunder-drummer-love-family-Rainbow Tribe—have grown so much as to overlap. You'll find a man doing shaman study involved with a men's group doing community drumming and so on.

VHB: *Like cells coming together*
AH: Right. These small underground cells have grown into a disease that's incurable once you get it. Part of my mission on the planet as I discover it (I don't really know what my mission is—whenever I think I do, it always surprises me) is being Arthur Rhythmseed. I'm going around showing how accessible it is, passing on this disease called *percussionitis*, which is incurable and contagious. The popularity, people going, "Wow, Look at this!" the overnight sensation of everybody discovering drumming as a tool, for one reason or another, has been a small, steady growth for twenty-five or thirty years. Baba Olatunji is finally getting the recognition he deserved thirty years ago. Baba isn't doing anything different or new. His mission has always been the same. What he has taught me is perseverance in truth and spirit.
VHB: *Yeah, I agree.*

AH: All of a sudden there's this overnight sensation that took twenty-five years to happen. A rediscovery of the drum as a tool for transformation, as a glue for unifying all people, all races, all genders, all religions. The drum has no color or philosophy. It is ultimate truth in the moment. And the quality of music of a drum circle is not necessarily created by the quality of the facilitator.

VHB: *(Laughter) Say a little more.*
AH: It's an illusion. The quality of a community drum circle is the quality of the alchemy of the participants. My job is not to create community or good music, but to help us facilitate ourselves to the place where spirit drops in and visits, and we are not playing, but being played. At that point, I am obsolete, and that's the time for me to move on to another circle. To lead others to lead themselves. Once the community gets it, they don't need someone standing in the middle.

VHB: *You make yourself obsolete in a wonderful way. Allowing the community to take over.*
AH: Other facilitators acknowledge the *percussionitis* in themselves. To enjoy it, they need to play with others. They enthuse others, teach what they know, so they can find out what they don't know, and create a drumming community because they're lonely.

VHB: *(laughter) You're right.*

AH: If you find yourself drumming in Siberia, you'll be the next facilitator for birthing that community. I've seen it happen in Idaho, Kansas, Pocatella, Podunk, anywhere. People end up creating their own drumming community. And it's easy. Go down to the nearest park, sit down and play. And if you're there every Saturday, guess what? It just starts growing.

VHB: *What advice do you have for beginning students?*

AH: Put the drum DOWN. Walk away. Go out in the universe. Open up your child's eyes. Look, listen, and feel all the rhythms that have BEEN THERE FOR ALL OF YOUR LIFE.

I have run into many students who learned drum rhythms from other teachers, and that's all they can play. They can't play their SELVES. No one taught them that the rhythms in their own universe are teachers, or how to access them.

Listen to a conversation between two people, without the words, and listen to the dance and song. It will tell you more than what the words mean.

I want to play with beginners in such a way, that not only can I teach them to play rhythms—as any drum teacher should, would and could—but also sit down with them and share our spirit together, outside of anything they might have learned or copied from some other culture.

VHB: *How do you see the evolution of drumming?*

AH: Two hundred years ago there was an island that was turned into a slave state, where people had been stolen from their (home) cultures. Only half that were stolen made it there alive. Though they all spoke different languages, they understood the universal language of the drum. Out of Spanish, indigenous Native American, and African cultures came a whole new culture where drumming was still a part of everyday life, in ritual, harvesting, marriage, birth, and death. And now two hundred years later it is a well-defined, developed drum culture based on a mixmatch and it's called Afro-Cuban.

The US is the biggest cultural mixing bowl: European, Turkish, African, Pakistani, Indian, Brazilian, Spanish, but we have lost our drums. For example: here's an AmericanIndian AfricanEuropean person. But what culture does he or she go back to?

What we should do, what we are doing is begin to build our own drumming culture, here in the U.S., using what we learn from other cultures that have not lost their drums.

Part of my mission is to help induce that, so that we can have our own drumming rituals—birthing, dancing, healing, transformation, harvesting, planting, whatever. Within two hundred years, and I'll be long dead before that happens, but it is part of this process that is now IRREVOCABLE.

We are now a drumming community in the United States. We are solidly on the path to grow, share, learn from, and respect representatives of cultures that are here to share *their* culture and spirit. At the same time we are here to be a part of taking back the drums. We, as European-Americans, lost our drums a long time before we started taking the drums away from others—during the Inquisition, the witch burnings, the gypsy burnings, the purges of the Druids.

What I am doing is building the larger drumming community, but that is the most gross and subtle aspect of what's going on.

VHB: *Thank you, Arthur. That was great.*

An Interview with Layne Redmond
Source: *Village Heartbeat*, Vol. 3, No. 1, February 1995

Layne Redmond is an educator of the power of the ancient feminine spirit through the use of the frame drum. She has compiled years of research in a book that will be released soon called "When the Drummers Were Women." She has been a student of Glen Velez on the frame drum and tambourine.

VHB: *What drew you into drumming?*
Layne: About fifteen years ago, I was drawn to learning to play the conga drum. I did that for a little while, and then I met my teacher Glen Velez, and played the Brazilian tambourine. So I began studying the various kinds of tambourines with him, and I never went back to the conga or any other kind of drum after that. I just stayed with the frame drum.

VHB: *Are you teaching from a Middle Eastern tradition?*
Layne: The technique is from the Middle East, but all the rhythms I am playing, all the ways I am teaching, are completely my own. In the Middle East, they would never stand or walk while they are playing. They sit in chairs, though there are traditions of playing in parades or processionals.

VHB: *What was it about the frame drum that was particularly potent for you?*
Layne: I don't even know. It didn't make sense. I was a visual artist and a performance artist. I had been pouring all my time into my art work and waitressing, then found that I was now studying

this instrument very seriously. It was a demand on my time that I couldn't rationalize.

I was torn for a long time. Then we started to record albums and do a lot of performing, and it slowly became the focus. Three or four years ago, I took my last art commission. Drumming has taken over my life.

VHB: *And Glen Velez has been your greatest influence?*
Layne: Oh yes, without a doubt. I've played with him for nine years.

VHB: *So how did you develop the style of playing that you teach?*
Layne: In the beginning, I was teaching mostly women, and I was drawn to teaching in a circle. I wanted them to experience the pulse by walking, have that be the base pulse in their bodies.

Sure I could take somebody, sit them down, show them how to play a rhythm on a frame drum, show them all the techniques, and they'll be able to play the rhythm. But it will have no connection to any kind of inner pulse. People who are just beginning aren't aware of that. Sometimes they are captivated by learning to play complex rhythms without having any sense of time.

I'm very interested in how people connect to their *own* sense of time and how that connects to a *group* shared sense of time. It's something that other cultures have not lost—people of Bali, India, Africa. There is a shared sense of pulse and rhythm that manifests in a community. People of European descent have definitely lost that quality.

VHB: *And do you find that your method is an easier way to get people in touch with it?*
Layne: I was trained as a tap dancer, which is serious rhythmic practice. I was also a cheerleader. Cheerleaders tend to be dismissed as superficial, but I realize now that I used rhythmic movement and chanting to rouse and shape group energy, to focus it, to get people entrained with me.

That's basically what I'm doing now, conveying and transmitting rhythmic information, almost directly to people's bodies. It's not a left-brain rational operation. I'm trying to teach mind-body synchronization, rhythmic unity. It might appear simplistic, but what's getting accomplished is not simplistic.

VHB: *Your teaching is unusual. Not only can you teach frame drum well, integrating the mind-body, but you also have developed, documented and researched a scholarly and theoretical approach to the origins and uses of the frame drum.*
Layne: It's interesting that you are asking me about this because I just started the plunge back into it. I spent six months last year completely

focused on writing this book, and I'm about to go back to being totally focused on it. That's what I've been doing all weekend.

It's been years of study. I've spent the last three or four years immersed in it when I'm not traveling or teaching and performing. Ten or eleven years ago, I began to organize the research Glen had collected. I noticed that there were all these goddesses playing frame drum, all these women. It became important for me to find out about that.

I've found amazing things from doing this research. There are no books on the frame drum. There is no history put together of the women who played these drums. I am compiling all this information from disparate sources like museums, archeological journals, picture collections, temple walls. A lot of this stuff isn't published.

You've got to go to the sites and see what's there. I travel a lot to Syria, Egypt, Cyprus, Greece, Sicily, Italy, and Turkey, to the main European countries that house most of the art, to Berlin, England and France to see their collections.

Particularly in Egypt I found a lot of images of women and the goddess Hathor and Isis playing the frame drum.

VHB: *Do you feel a connection with that [the past images of women as drummers]?*

Layne: I certainly do. As is always the case, you find that your life is a mirror for a lot of these things. There are many similarities and environments, many coincidences and chances that bring you into this material, then into understanding what the material represents. I had no basis to judge my own abilities when I began playing because Glen didn't have long-term students. Now that I have spent a lot of time teaching, I realize that I was extremely talented however you want to define talent. It wasn't something I was aware of at the time. I had a lot of innate capacity to do this. I had a lot of facility with my fingers and I had a lot of rhythmic training and a natural sense of connection to rhythm. I realize that I have a lot of ability to do this. When I see the reaction people have to women with the same capacity, I say, "of course, they are all reincarnated frame drummers."

I do remember pieces, and the pieces that I compose or write seem to come to me when I play the drum, and I think I remember them, hear them, and seem to recapture them.

VHB: *You have been in drumming for a long time. How do you view the current growing interest in drumming?*

Layne: It's amazing. When I started playing these drums, I was just in Glen's apartment. We played for years without people even being aware of us. Slowly people started being aware of frame drums and it spread into the world of percussion and now it's phenomenal. It's not like I thought fifteen years ago, "I'm going to take up frame drums and it's going to be a great career."

I've gotten real interested in incenses from the ancient world and aromatherapy. Those who are very involved in aromatherapy, you know the same thing must have happened to them 15 or 20 years ago. They found themselves interested in something unusual and now there's great interest and awareness.

I could never have foretold what would be going on now, never, ever. There is a musical group, the Anonymous Four, who are playing early medieval and Renaissance music, Gregorian chants. All of a sudden this group, the music is becoming very popular. They are bestsellers now.

People want to reconnect to music on an intimate level, they want to be participants, not to listen to recorded music. They want to make music themselves. They want to play and hear acoustic instruments.

Drumming in particular has a real meaning for the development of community. People working together, moving together, having a unified experience, and it's also the basis of community ritual.

VHB: *That's wonderful. I noticed that when you play the frame drum you can't overpower each other.*
Layne: No you can't. It's not about hitting the drum. It's about using all your fingers. You really cannot hit the frame drum.

VHB: *How does the rise of African drumming play into your world of frame drums?*
Layne: It does not work too well to have frame drums play with an African ensemble. However, if you have a sensitive drummer anything is possible.

I think when people first get drawn to African drums, there is a physical energy thing that goes along with that, so there might not be so much listening that goes on. But I don't have much experience with that. I haven't studied African drumming at all. The frame drum is a very soft instrument. Also it demands facility in your hands.

Anybody becoming a master drummer of any type of African style—that's years of rigorous study and practice, which is no different from mastering a frame drum. Initially, anyone can stand in front of an African drum and bring their hands down on it. With a frame drum, first you've got to hold it in one hand and differentiate all your fingers. It's more problematic to introduce it to people than to introduce them to an African drum. They can get much more juice back from an African drum than they can get from a frame drum. That's why I start everybody on the tambourine, because it's the most user-friendly of all frame drums. You've got the jingles, it's wonderful, you can get so many different sounds and then put it in your pocketbook and take it anywhere in the world with you.

VHB: *What gender issues have come up for you in the drumming world?*

Layne: When I was first playing, I was playing with Glen, and like I said, I didn't study music or have musical education. Glen did, went to a conservatory, and studied percussion. All the people around him had done the same—very educated percussionists. Then we had a trio with Steve Gorn, another master musician, and I found myself with two master musicians and I felt I could never match up or measure up. But I thought, "What can I bring to this music that we are making?" It wasn't a conscious thing that I could bring a sense of primordial feminine energy. I didn't think it out and say "What's that?" and "How can I develop this?" But that was the difference and that's what I could bring. A lot of the exercises that I taught in my workshop about connecting to the earth and bringing the energy up and radiating it out, that was how I developed that.

I'm fairly proficient, but there are other people a lot more proficient than I am on frame drums. But there is something that happens when I play that really affects people. There is an energy generated. But I am always having to deal with the fact that I am in a profession that is mostly men, and that I never quite had the background or experience. It's been pointed out to me that if I had, I wouldn't have developed the kinds of things that I have developed.

VHB: *Thank you.*

An Interview with Mestre Beicola
Source: Village Heartbeat, Vol 6, No. 4, September 1998

Mestre Beicola is a master of capoeira, an African-Brazilian martial art and dance form. Now based in East Palo Alto, California, Beiçola has performed and taught capoeira, Brazilian dance, percussion, and stringed instruments at Stanford, UC Berkeley, and throughout the world. A native of Rio de Janeiro, Brazil, Beiçola first came to the United States in 1988 with the samba extravaganza "Oba Oba," a company of 70 top Brazilian musicians, capoeiristas and dancers. He continues to instruct hundreds of students in the South Bay at his Brazivedas home-studio.

VHB: *So let's start at the beginning. You got into capoeira because of your father?*

MB: Yes, my father was a capoeirista. He wasn't a master or a formal teacher. He taught me when I was very small. I was so young that I didn't remember my father teaching me. My son is the same way. He doesn't remember me touching him this way, flipping him. He thinks he learned it by himself.

My father was a street fighter, and because he didn't want me to follow in his footsteps, he stopped teaching me. When I was twelve, I moved to another neighborhood that was a little more dangerous in a complex of buildings. All of a sudden, I was aware of capoeira, thinking about it, but I never remembered seeing it before. What I learned from my father came back to me. I had some friends and we messed around and we didn't know anything. I started to search and met some people who knew something about capoeira, but they didn't want anyone to know…their secret self-defense. They didn't advertise, because the neighborhood is dangerous. You began to see that there is a way that a capoeirista walks, the way they look, and you say, "You know capoeira."

I started to train by myself. I was twelve, and my friend would bring capoeiristas to me, so I could learn, and sure enough one day he brought someone who could really teach me. I began to train and in a year, I started to teach. In Brazil all the kids play soccer and so I would take the soccer ball and say, "No, today we're going to do capoeira." We would do a half hour and I'd give the soccer ball back. Some kids stayed with soccer, some went with capoeira. That's how my first group started, in the grass in my back yard behind my building.

I learned a lot by watching. I didn't have the money, so I would go to the classes to watch. Afterwards I would go home and train everything that I saw. The class finishes at eleven and at home I would be training until one in the morning so I wouldn't forget.

You can go to the beach and play capoeira. My main goal was to go to the beach, get beat up a little bit, go in the water and let the salt water heal things, see if my body is OK, go home. One day I could play capoeira and no one could touch me any more. On Sunday, we would go to this place where all the great capoeiristas in the country go. I wanted to play and asked my teacher. At first he said no, but then he asked me if I thought I could take care of myself. I said yes and he said go. I was so strong that a teacher came to me and said, "Where do you come from? I am going to be opening a school and I want you to help me." So I did. I learned even more at that school and became his student, but I never had to pay to learn because I was assisting. It paid for a master's degree in capoeira.

VHB: *Then what?*
MB: At seventeen, I went to the army in Brazil. Everyone goes. I liked it. I was outdoors. I trained all the time. Brazil never goes to war and so I exercised, worked in the kitchen. I was doing capoeira in the Army the whole time, training people. I took a test to become a sergeant and advanced. I was the youngest sergeant in Brazil. I was so proud. I knew everything! I was there seven years.

VHB: *When you studied capoeira formally, did you learn the berimbau and all too?*
MB: Yeah, but when I grew into my capoeira, no one taught me anything. I just learned by looking. My father was a musician and I was always around the music. I would go to shows and I would look at how the guy was playing the *pandeiro*, and I would pay attention to the technique. I would start to play on my leg so I wouldn't forget, then go home and practice playing the cooking pans. Because I grew up with the rhythm, I could tell whether the rhythm was right or not. I could just hear it. The thing about Brazil is that as you grow up and the music is right there, you put your hands out and start to play. And when you're playing wrong, people tell you. If you continue to play, they get mad. First, they try to take the instrument out of your hands. If you keep coming back and persist, they will show you. I started to learn music by hanging out with a lot of people. First, you start with one group and as you improve, the groups change. The group I used to hang out with are now all professional singers and musicians.

VHB: *What about after the army?*
MB: When I got done with the army, I worked out a lot, from 8 to 5 every single day at the gym. I didn't want to compete. I had to work too hard! I wanted to do this for fun, not for the competition aspect. One year, my students were bothering me so much about this capoeira tournament in Rio de Janeiro that I participated, won, and never competed any more!

VHB: *I am curious about how the Escuela da Samba started?*
MB: Everything came from slave time when the slaves, mainly the Congolese, liked to get together and play drums. (It's the Bantu people that influenced the capoeira world.) When slavery ended they still got together to play drums. They liked to imitate the noblemen, so the Carnival was a time when they dressed up as King and Queen. Also, the noblemen could dress any way that they wanted and would mix with the people.

VHB: *How did Carnival get started?*
MB: In the beginning, it started with the neighborhoods, or with the tribe or a small village.

It was first called *bloco*. The people in the neighborhood would make a costume parade for the community. It wasn't a competition. The community would go parade in other communities and that's how the whole thing started. Afterwards, it became a competition with prizes. People began to invest more. Someone figures they can make money making costumes and everything builds. Out of that came the whole idea of Samba school. You are in the neighborhood and you start to compete and as you win you more up, up, up. The city started to organize. The groups started to parade downtown and you end up with a Samba school with 4,000 members. People bring in their whole family and friends, and generations follow.

VHB: *Is there some connection to religion?*
MB: Yes, it comes from a religious tradition. During the four days of Carnival you can do whatever you want, all kinds of crazy stuff. You can dress like a woman, have affairs, people kill people—so many things happen. On Ash Wednesday, you are supposed to burn your costume and for forty days you are not supposed to play music, no radio—just pray. That's the way it used to be, but now no one pays attention. They announce the results of the winners on Thursday but Saturday and Sunday the parades begin again. What I like best about Carnival is the preparation. The whole of Brazil is really happy. They start to prepare in August and by December the whole place is on fire.

VHB: *So you like to take people to Brazil for the Carnival time?*
MB: People were so amazed at the San Francisco Carnival that I wanted to show them the real thing. I wanted to show some of my students how they do the costumes, how to get ideas, so I started to take my students to Brazil. This year is my fifth year. I take them to Rio and Bahia to take classes, to learn about the culture, and to take part in Carnival. In Rio, they get the big Carnival and we also go to Bahia because it is the center of Africa in Brazil. It's amazing what you find there!

VHB: *Is there racial tension in Brazil?*
MB: The racial tension is different. It is very strong and very subtle. If you are not in the middle class, you don't confront it. The way you are brought up in Brazil, since the time you are a kid, you are told (and of course it is not true) that white people are better. You are trained to be housecleaners or to work in a car wash. It is so subtle, you don't realize it. You would go downtown and be afraid to stop in front of a hotel. The TV, the movies, were only white people. You grow up with it every single day and you think this is

the way the world works. There are still places where black people cannot go into white clubs, but whites can go to blacks—so it is not racist. Brazil was colonized differently than America. Here they had the intentions to colonize, in Brazil to exploit. The government mentality was different. The separation came from the noble family. At the level of the working class they have no power. In the high positions in Brazil you don't see many black people. Except in the army, but not in aeronautics.

When I grew up, there was either Jimmy Brown (James Brown soul music) or rock 'n' roll. People would fight and say rock 'n' roll was for whites. No, rock 'n' roll was for blacks. The government came in and said, "OK, here's disco…" and that was for everyone. Now, Brazilian music is very popular. In the past it was only American music. Now everybody mixes—black and white—to learn the samba.

VHB: *Thank you.*

An Interview with Zorina Wolf
Source: *Village Heartbeat*, Vol. 3, No. 5, January 1996

In a reversal of roles, Zorina Wolf has agreed to switch interview seats and share her own experiences about drumming, community, and her recent trip to Ghana.

VHB: *A few years ago, you were on course to become a spiritual teacher—a rabbi. Now you are teaching drumming. How did you make this jump?*
Z: Well, actually, both paths were riding in tandem for quite some time. One summer three years ago, I went from an eight-day workshop with Baba directly to this very big deal Jewish renewal forum, and I guess it was there that it became obvious to me that the Judaic style of prayer was too limiting for me. I wanted to rewrite the liturgy. And in order to do that, I would have had to become a scholar. Instead I became more deeply drawn to the immediacy of drumming as my spiritual path.

VHB: *What is your vision for community drumming?*
Z: First, I envision a community. Now it's not so much of what it looks like, it's that it is. In my heart of hearts I would like to see the world of ritual as part of that community as well—that we can develop ways of using the natural cycles in

life, so that we remember that we are alive. That's all it is. To give praise and thanks together, using drumming as a means of expressing the event, whether it's the full moon, or birthdays, deaths, all the human events we could celebrate, creating theater, ritual, dance, all with drumming. Sometimes I see that as being here, other times I feel that this vision may be still a ways off. We may be too defended still to be able to enact that in a group. That's what happens sometimes at drum circles. We need to identify ourselves as individuals inside a group. And so does everyone else, myself included. So, it gets noisy sometimes.

VHB: Do you consider yourself a preservationist?
Z: What do you mean by that? Do you mean do I have a vested interest in seeing the culture that drumming came from preserved? Yes, I do, although I wonder about it, too. I believe very deeply for myself that rhythms are the keys to deep knowledge. Often times when we are learning a traditional rhythm, we can get the notes right, but the feeling inside the music might not be there yet. I know there are a lot of folks out there that don't understand that. You've either got the notes or you don't. But I am talking about the magic, the medicine, the vibrational healing that is present in these very old rhythms that originated sometimes from the shrine. That's something. I personally want to be humble enough around that spirit world to receive whatever it is willing to give me, for clarity, strength, healing. Some people believe that there is no spirit world. For them the notion of some other unseeables is not so. Well, OK, look, there is that possibility, but I'd rather live from a place where I had to give it up to someone, something else, than assume I am the only center for knowledge or wisdom. So yeah I am [a preservationist]. I want to carry the messages taught to me with a lot of respect. Who was here first? It wasn't me.

VHB: *There seem to be so many components to drumming, and so many reasons people drum. Do we each need to focus on all of them when we drum together? How much awareness is needed?*
Z: I think the main thing for me is to be open to what I don't know. That cultivates an attitude that makes it easier to learn, easier to receive. The other thing is that we need each other. One drum is wonderful. By ourselves, for our own meditation and entertainment. But we need each other for the music. It's like Sanga was saying, that the person sitting next to you, well you might hate them in "real" life, but inside drumming you love that person, you need them and their energy and their strength to help you to stay on track. Then they become your best friend. Beyond that, the drum has its own path for each of us. Again I say the main thing to be aware of is that it is a powerful vehicle, and whatever way you are drumming, you need to recognize that from time to time.

VHB: *Do you believe that politics comes with the drumming territory?*

Z: I do believe there is, oh yes. Do I want there to be, no. But I am not a political person. I don't like power brokering. I am too scared for that. It gives me paranoid feelings. But it's there. There is a need to recognize and honor our drumming elders and teachers and give credit where credit is due—they stuck it out and became drummers. In that situation the politics are about doing the right thing, regardless of how you might feel about that person personally. But lobbying for power, there is enough to go around. We are our own worst enemies in bondage to the ego when we don't want to praise someone because it might take away something from ourselves.

VHB: *What needs to happen for a drum circle to work, given that there are so many different abilities, intensities, and types of drums and percussion?*

Z: Some strong drummers who can hold a variety of parts, including and most necessarily the bottom. Everyone wants to solo—not that many of us have anything that profound to say. It's great when the spirit takes you and you are wailing away, but I don't feel as if I have the skill yet to express myself the way I want to, so I play the bottom, play the cowbell with a nice solid clave to hold the whole glue of it together. Also to teach the beginners the bottom as well so they are contributing in a very important way to the music. Solo for a short time, then come back to earth. And again, I say with great reverence, watch the volume. If you can't hear the person sitting next to you, that's a clue.

VHB: *What impressions did you bring back from Ghana?*

Z: Ghana! What can I say about a two-week trip to Africa? I loved being there. Two weeks is only a short time, and it is a very long time as well, enough to get a feeling for the incredible richness the continent of Africa presents. There were sixteen of us who went to Ghana in late August on a tour that Baba Olatunji arranged. We were students at the International Centre for African Music and Dance, which was under the umbrella of the University of Ghana. We were in some ways protected from the intensity of Accra by being in an academic setting.

At the same time, we were thrown into a treasure trove of the repertoire of Ghanaian music and dance as displayed almost every day by the Ghanaian Dance Ensemble. We were surrounded by music. It is everywhere. I was struck over and over again by the musical power and knowledge inside every culture. In Ghana there are three main groups that I was aware of—the Akan, the Ga and the Ewe—and a lot of subgroups inside each of them. That's a lot of music to be exposed to.

VHB: *Thank you, Zorina.*

Interview with Malidoma and Sobunfu Somé,
Source: Village Heartbeat, Vol 2, No. 5, December 1994

Malidoma and Sobonfu Somé are two teachers of the art of indigenous ritual and spirituality. Although Malidoma was educated in a Western tradition, holding doctorates from the Sorbonne and Brandeis University, he returned to the village of his birth in Burkina Faso when he was twenty and underwent a traditional Dagara initiation to reintegrate himself with his ancestral spirits. Malidoma uses the tools of our society to present the deep spirituality of African culture. He has written three books: Ritual: Power, Healing and Community, Of Water and Spirit, *and* The Healing Wisdom of Africa. *Shortly before this interview with Village Heartbeat he had given a presentation at the Afro-American Center in San Jose.*

VHB: *What is it like for both you and Sobonfu to have a foot in two worlds, both the world of traditional ritual and this Western, modern world?*
Malidoma: It is a very, very strange and delicate dance that requires constant awareness. You can't go to sleep, because you never know in what kind of state you are going to wake. That is the most compelling part. However, there is a positive part that allows for tremendous learning, by comparison and contrast, because what is hard to understand in one place can be a lot easier in another.

I know that the modern logical world is extremely hard to handle, impossible to handle. So the best way to approach it is from underground. It is impossible to go out there parading defiantly of the practical physical world, in this modern state.

Even though it looks like we are moving with one foot in one world and one foot in the other, the only way we can survive is to stay most of the time in the spirit world, in a place that has ritual quality, a place that allows for constant check-up with spirit in order to have a way of saying that we are being guided by the spirit behind whatever we are doing.

VHB: *So even in the midst of all your technical learning and degrees, you have been able to keep your place in the world of spirit?*
Sobonfu: Without this it would be pretty hard to accomplish anything, without the spiritual connection it would feel like disconnecting from the village again. I don't think one can really survive as a normal person.
M: The tendency is for people to see these things as separate and antithetical, as if one is allergic to

another. But the material world is just a part of the spirit that it deserted. If you want to function in it successfully, you have to load up a great deal of spirit energy so that you maneuver in it. If you enter completely naked, you can only be battered and abused and constantly beaten up by it, and that includes any person who even looks successful in it. Maneuvering properly in the modern world doesn't mean you have control of it.

S: That's right.

M: Because modern means an energy that has gone astray, that has gone wild, is not reconciled.

S: …and is going to divide and conquer you. I think that the spiritual message is something that you have to keep no matter how lonely it makes you feel and how awkward you look to other people, something I don't think I can personally live without.

VHB: *It can be difficult to operate inside this thing called community in the West. We don't seem to have a direct interdependence on one another that you can trace. We are interdependent, of course, but sometimes we don't perceive this, and the end result is isolation. How does this compare to where you come from?*

M: The very reason that people experience isolation is they have run out of the dynamic that used to be the sustaining force of the indigenous world. Modern means something that has cut away itself from the indigenous rhythm of life. I'm not talking about indigenous that is articulated in terms of primitivism, that is to say architecturally, technologically, and so and so, I'm talking about indigenous spiritually. When that kind of spirit is not there, isolation becomes the replacing system. It is important to know, at least from the tribe, this kind of isolation is totally alien and completely absent simply because of the very kind of way the whole indigenous structure is built.

When you know you live in a large family of several dozens of people, you share the same community place, most of the time, no one has a private room. Rooms are for several people at a time. It is hard to really speak of isolation. What are you isolated from, really? Here we have the privatization of everything. My room has to have a door, my apartment has to have a door and I have to carry the key. Everybody you see outside of their homes, if you ask them, "Do you have your keys," they will show you keys to the house.

In the village, if you said to someone, "Show me the keys to your house," he or she would never have heard of anything like that. That person may be away from home, but there are plenty of people who live at home, and there is a constant feeling of linkage.

In order to talk about us, you have to go that far and be that down-to-earth to see what is constant isolation. That is why when you wake up into the spirit, after this kind of circumstance, you have big trouble.

S: When I first got here, we had a big apartment, just Malidoma and myself. Once people in the village heard that, they got really scared. Were we really OK? Because to have a house with just two people is unthinkable. It feels like something is wrong, and something *is* wrong. Because if you are alone and your energy is dissipated, and you don't have other people to be there for you, it's really hard to be in the community. You end up isolating yourself. When I first got here, it seemed like I could never ever have a community here.

VHB: *Do you feel like you have a community now?*
S: I feel like I'm beginning to have a community.
M: A community is a bunch of people who are around you in your life and are ready to intervene in support of whatever it is you are doing. In a lot of ways, there is indeed that. Being so far away, there is always going to be a margin of isolation. There is no way it can be replaced fully, because there is no way people can experience total connection in a culture that has made division a way of life.

VHB: *And also excluded ritual.*
M: That is something we cannot deny, or we'll become some kind of New-Agey loonies who say that everything is fine.
VHB: *What happened or called to you to share this wisdom with others in the West?*

M: It has to do with the kind of relationship we have with the people back home. We wouldn't just pack up and come over here, and decide to live the way we live without something having actually happened in the village. When we got the clear signal, the elders trusted us to be the translators of the wisdom they have lived by for thousands and thousands of years. There are two attitudes there. You can say "I can't do this," or you can go ahead, try it out, and see it as another form of initiation, where you are constantly sent somewhere where no elder will be guiding you directly in the field. You find that you have to return once in a while to get reoriented in order to get back to work. So we're not doing it because we tumbled onto it, we're doing it because we are responding directly to this strong recommendation or this strong order from our elders.
S: One of the things for me that is my purpose is to help uphold the knowledge of the ancestors, and also by working with Malidoma, but I knew that when we were together, I would have to uphold that.

VHB: *So you are the messengers. If someone from this society wanted to "work" to contact or connect with spirit, what could they do?*
M: It would depend on the individual. It's going to have to start with personal prayers and personal ritual. When you wake up to spirit, you

cannot act like someone who is waking up from a dream and therefore saying, "Hmmm, that's kind of strange, that's kind of interesting and blah blah blah…." This attitude does not constitute a dialogue with the very situation that one is in. Everyone knows how to pray. Everyone knows how to speak to spirit in terms of trying to align with something that is being witnessed or being experienced. A person who wakes up in spirit has to first begin with talking to that spirit, just verbalizing what is going on. That's a good start. You don't need to be an expert to do this kind of thing. After a while, you notice that some changes are happening, and eventually the spirit that is working with you will take you to the right places at the right time in order to do the right thing. I don't know of any other way. You cannot just go out in some kind of contemplative lifestyle into the bush, because sooner or later you're going to come back to town.

S: And something I feel is important is the existence of shrines as knowledge. The mention of shrines sometimes scares people away, but it has to start there, reconnecting with the ancestors and asking them, "What should I do now, where should I go?"

VHB: *And how do people hear the answers?*
M: The answers are not heard the way we hear a message from the TV. They can be heard as a form of conviction. It starts with a little bit of trust. It seems as though people find it very hard to trust anything, especially something that does not obey the logic that is current. This is not something that can be taught and broken down into pieces. People just have to trust that what they are seeing is not an illusion, that there is some concrete reality attached to it, even though they are not able to explain it in detail. If they don't want to do that, if they can't do that, it means that they are in for a very heavy-duty initiation, because when you wake up you can't go back to sleep again. That's hard. It's good news for people who are looking forward to waking up, but bad news for those who thought they were better off staying asleep.

VHB: *Is there a difference between rituals for men and women?*
S: There are kinds of rituals women do in the village that are not only for women and the kinds of rituals that men do are not only for men. That's one of the first differences and the other difference is…I don't know if there is any difference in how we go to spirit. We all go with sincerity. It's the heart that matters. If you want to discuss how men and women grieve, that's another thing. Women channel up energy constantly, it's in their bones, everybody knows that. And men have an easier time grieving once they are in a ritual space.

VHB: *Thank you both.*

Interview with Samba Ngo
Source: Village Heartbeat, Vol 3, No. 2, March/April 1995

Samba Ngo is international musician and performer. He was born in Zaire and moved to the Congo when he was young. He is recording a new album in France and the US that will be released in 2016. He is a skilled composer, guitarist, singer, kalimba player, and a great guy. Here is an interview written in 1995.

VHB: *I want to ask you how it was that you came to be a musician. How did you first come to understand music?*
Samba: I don't really have a memory of a time or a moment. I have a memory of it always being like that for me. As soon as I had the ability to play an instrument, I played that instrument. This is *kalimba* (thumb piano), this was my first instrument, but there was not a moment. My whole village is a music village, with colorful people, with musicians coming from everywhere and passing through. When I began to travel with the band of the village, I saw things that I had never seen, other instruments, different things, different music. I didn't really begin at the beginning. I was beginning since I'm born. I was born in Zaire, and then my mother sent me to a school in the Congo. (*How far away is that?* Oh, that's way across the river. It's another country.)

Over there, I was part of the activities, a dance group, playing a little bit. I used to make drums, but my focus was on school. I would travel again to the village, back to Congo, finally to France, then the United States, and I am here.

VHB: *So you started with the kalimba. Do you have a reputation as a kalimba player?*
Samba: No, because when I got with Titos' band (Titos Sompa), I used to play the *kalimba* for a few songs, but the guitar attracted me because I am from the village. My whole energy began to go to the guitar...less energy in the *kalimba*.

VHB: *Was it a natural transition in some way because they are both percussion instruments?*
Samba: Yes, for me I always tried to make sounds on the guitar like that of traditional instruments. I never went to school to learn to play like Jimi Hendrix. Me, I follow how the traditional instrument sounds. I am more familiar with that, and that is the way my style began. I have part city man because I am a city man and I have part

village because I am of the village. I have the influence of living in Europe for a long time, and I put those expressions in the music.

When I read what the music journalists write about my music, they say "It's jazz, it's jazz-rock, it's world beat, it's soukous." I try to use the whole thing that Africa has, and when you listen to it with modern ears, you'd say, "This rhythm is funky." In Africa, we have that thing in our music. And we have many traditional albums, CDs and whatever to prove what I am saying.

In my conviction, it's impossible for somebody to say, "OK, I am a musician." No, it's up to music to choose you. You have that in your blood. It's not every African that is a musician, but the majority of the Africans have contact with the rhythm. It is our culture. It's like Frances Bebe says, "Music is not a part of life, it is the life itself of the African."

Somebody dies, is born, whatever, there is a song for that, a dance, a way of expression. But it's not like here, in the Occident the music is not like that, where the music is used for the creation, not for the transformation. That is the difference.

But every culture has those elements, in this culture it's just a question of how you are going to wake them up. Now you see that almost everywhere, people have the drum. You see these circles here, and as you said, it didn't used to be like that. That means that something has changed. Something is moving. More people travel and so there are more people in quantity influencing the quality of life.

VHB: *I want to introduce a broader understanding of the kalimba for our audience.*

Samba: The teaching of the *kalimba*…maybe it would be better to perhaps use a different word, because you cannot teach the *kalimba* in three hours. It is an approach. The *kalimba* represents a big culture, besides the *kalimba* itself. In South Africa, for example, in the ethnic culture of the Lemba from Transvaal, the *kalimba* is a sacred instrument. In the mythology of those people, the king becomes *kalimba*. In other cultures it is not only the radio, but also an instrument to cure. In some countries they use a harp. Every country uses a different instrument. Kalimba for the Lemba, and I use them as an example because it is a part of the kingdom, the power. But also the instrument in Africa represents something very deep.

VHB: *Thank you.*

An Interview with Sule Greg Wilson
Source: Village Heartbeat, Vol 2, No, 3 June 1994

Greg Wilson is author of *The Drummer's Path: Moving the Spirit with Ritual and Traditional Drumming.*

VHB: *As I understand it, your book (The Drummer's Path) is the first of its kind to be a teaching text for drummers, to give an overview of the path of drumming. What are three pieces of information that a drummer, or a beginning drummer, should know?*
Sule: If you want to get real basic, the most important thing is how you stand. The breathing comes out of the posture, like that. That's one.

Number two is understanding that each drum is its own voice, is its own culture, is its own thing. You have to make a relationship with each instrument, with each orchestra of instruments, with each family of instruments. A *donno* is not a *dundun* is not a *tama*, although everybody would call all of them talking drum. A viola is not a violin, even though they look similar. That's two.

And three, when you're drumming, it brings forth your solar force when you play. It does that to everyone. So people need to temper that with their lunar force, otherwise they'll just become arrogant. They also must foster their Venusian force to learn how to work with people. And then you must get your transcendent force so you can use all those for the good of everybody.

VHB: *When you set out to find out these things for yourself, who was your biggest influence?*
Sule: God (laughs). The world. I didn't set out to do it. I've been there. It's a spiritual thing. It's not about being a musician. It's about using the stuff to get the spiritual point across, to get the world harmonized. So you don't necessarily go to musicians for that. I've had lots of mentors—priest mentors, homeless people mentors, bad musician mentors, good musician mentors, relatives and friends. The records I listened to were Santana and Olatunji and *Les Ballets Africains*. And then to Malo and Eddie Palmieri and Jimi Hendrix.

VHB: *You tell a story in your book about when you were back home and you heard some people playing for a class of dancers. But they were playing the rhythms differently from the way you had learned them, so you left. You said you learned an important lesson from that incident. Can you share that?*
Sule: Well, there were a couple of lessons from that. Number one, you have to accept people where they are, and don't try to push yourself

onto them. Let them enjoy themselves for who they are. That again is getting about being fundamental, as opposed to solar, 'cause that's the down side of the king [referring to solar energy as the kingly force]. You'll tell people what to do. And beyond being a king, you understand to let people be and they'll come along as fast as they can come along. That's one thing I learned, not to have to force people to play the way I thought was right. And the other thing I learned was that when you're in a certain place, you're in that place. If my energy level is going at a higher rate of vibration than theirs, that's just the way it is. And there I am. And there they're not.

VHB: *But you're both in the same place?*
Sule: No, you're both in the same space.

VHB: *physical space….*
Sule: But not the same rate of vibration. As I demonstrated in that workshop on djembe, the level of energy, of intensity that has to be there to play correctly, instantaneously. Like turning a laser on and off, not like lighting a candle and blowing it out. So I was there, and I was in a different place, and I had to accept where I was and accept where they were and let them be where they were, not to try to make them be where I was. One of those 'you can't go home again' kind of things.

VHB: *There is a place in one's learning where you've gone beyond bare bones beginner and you think you know a little something. Sometimes I think that's the most dangerous place to be because it would be very easy to do some social wrong without realizing it just by an assumption that "I've been studying this…."*
Sule: Therefore I know it. Well, I've done that and there are some occasions where I've done that and it's returned to me, and reminded me not to be there again. Because the lessons that I have learned are applications I have to make every time I have to go and learn something. That's why you don't necessarily have to learn from the best drummers, just those who have a right feeling for playing. And to tell you the truth, you don't know anything so you have to eat everything. You know something and you want to eat that, make everything taste like that. As you absorb that you realize that you don't know anything again. And once you know that, it comes back to you through the world, that you do know a lot, much more than many other people, but so does everyone else.

VHB: *So in essence you've said that everything is your learning place, not just your drum teacher or drum setting…that everything is teaching you about drumming.*
Sule: We had a rehearsal, we're getting ready to go to the studio, night before the rehearsal people want to start changing up arrangements (this is a band, this is not the *Drummer's Path* stuff). I was

highly upset. But by a year later, people are looking at me saying, "What's going on? You're not getting upset, you're not yelling and jumping up and down." I was totally calm, and as soon as the big somebody called it, I was ready to go. I was right there, 5,6,7,8, boom. Because I had realized my sense of responsibility toward myself was the ultimate thing, and the group can only go as far as everybody in the group can go. So if they're gonna freak out, they've got to freak out on their own. I mean if you're trying to stop them from freaking out, it will only give them more energy to freak out with.

That applies when somebody is playing solo, and they go just a little bit too far and they wind up being a little bit off of the clave [the beat]. The best thing to do is just (pause)…it's a funny place between holding your breath and deepening your breath to keep you from getting knocked off when they fall off the clave. So you just do that, and everything else will be just like putting a magnet underneath a piece of paper that has iron filings on it. Everything will just line up.

VHB: *That's a great way of putting it, and that leads perfectly into my next question, which is about soloing. You have a drum circle of twenty people or so. How does someone step out and solo?*
Sule: First is I'd tell everybody else to come down [in volume]. They have a council stick, everybody else pays attention, everybody else supports. And everybody plays to see how what they're doing fits with what the soloist is doing. 'Cause the soloist's responsibility is to pick out people that they are playing with, and talk to them. Your responsibility is to find the person that is most insecure, and play right along with them, the same thing that they are playing, until they are rock solid. And then you play the opposite of what they are playing, while you are looking at each other, so they can find the magic of communication. If you've got twenty people, and one person goes around the circle and does that with everybody, everybody will feel like they're having a good time. And that person doing the soloing will learn so much, and so will everybody else. Because you have to take your energy, put it into the other person, lock with theirs, just as if you have a loop of rope you put around both of your waists. And after you two have played together for a while, both of you lean back and create the tension between the two, both of you are locked in.

The soloist knows what I mean when I say to play the opposite part. Because when you have so many people of varying levels, you don't want to try to do a solo that's playing off the clave, because the fundamental is gonna be so taken up and there are going to be so many fill notes around the melody given that there are so many people, it's…I don't think doing that's a good idea. It's best to just look in on somebody's part and then highlight one another and another and that way everybody feels it better.

VHB: *For my personal information, did you receive a lot of response about what you had written about women drumming in the Drummer's Path?*
Sule: Not as much as I expected. It's so simple. Women have to do their own thing, men have to do their own thing. Who is going to do the playing? Hello! I wish I had more time and information. I spoke to a woman drummer and said, "Yeah, go play your *djembe*, just to prove that you can play the *djembe*, but why aren't any women playing women's drums? So busy trying to prove you can play as well as men, why don't you play some women's drums? Or let the men play the women's drums and see what happens."

VHB: *What are the women's drums?*
Sule: I have pictures in the book of tambourines and frame drums and bones, and there are calabash drums. There are all different ways of playing calabash drums, either as water drums, or playing the gourds themselves, which men and women do, or playing the skins on the gourds, carved wooden drums, bowl wooden drums, which I've seen pictures of women playing. I've seen photos of women playing different kinds of bells, net drums, kinda like a *sekere*, pictures of women playing these huge friction drums, playing different kinds of marimba stuff, *makquiasno*.

VHB: *You're saying, find out more about what harmonizes with you as a woman, what nurtures you?*
Sule: Yeah, well, calabash is a universal symbol. When women play these it's interesting. Take a bag of cowries, throw it in the air, and it's a woman's drum. There is a book, *The Heart of the Forest*, where the Baka women are playing water, standing in the water, drumming on the water while they sing.

VHB: *Thank you, Sule*

Glossary

Ase or *Ashe* (ah-SAY or ah-SHAY): A Yoruba word meaning power, command, and authority. The ability to make whatever one says happen. Often summarized as "so be it," "so it is," or "it definitely shall be so." I've also heard it said that the quality of *ase* is like cool water poured over the top of your head on a hot day.

Atabaque (atabaki): A tall, wooden, Afro-Brazilian hand drum. The shell is made traditionally of Jacaranda wood from Brazil. The head is traditionally made from calfskin.

Bell or *agogô* or *gankogui*: An instrument played with a stick. *Agogo* is a Yoruba word meaning bell. *Gankogui* is from Ghana. The bell had its origin in traditional Yoruba music and also in samba *baterias* (percussion ensembles), but now it is used throughout the world. Now bells can be manufactured and come in a variety of pitches.

Berimbau: A single-string percussion instrument, a musical bow, from Brazil. Originally from Africa, the *berimbau* was eventually incorporated into the practice of the Afro-Brazilian martial art, *capoeira*. It is made from the wood of a *beriba* tree, a steel string, and a *cabasa* or half gourd. The gourd is hollowed out, dried and attached to the lower portion of the bow with a string that acts as a resonator.

Bottom part: The essential part of any rhythm orchestration. The "engine" that moves the train of the entire rhythm.

Calypso: Calypso is a style of Afro-Caribbean music that originated in Trinidad and Tobago during the early to mid-20th century and was popularized in the U.S. by Harry Belafonte. One of his most popular tunes is "Day O," released in 1956. Calypso rhythms can be traced back to West African Kaiso and the arrival of French planters and their slaves in the 1700s.

Chops: Technical ability and flair on the drum or any other instrument.

Clave: *Clave* is a Spanish word meaning "code" or "key," as in key to a mystery or puzzle. In drumming it means the key rhythm pattern. Claves are also resonant percussive sticks. The bell plays the clave (the key rhythm pattern), and claves (sticks) can also play the clave (the key rhythm pattern).

Conga: 1) A rhythm that is played with a conga line. 2) A tall, narrow, single-headed drum from Cuba. Congas are staved like barrels and classified into three types: *quinto* (lead drum, highest), *conga* (middle), and *tumbao* (lowest). Congas are traditionally used in Afro-Cuban genres.

Cross rhythm or polyrhythm: Two different rhythmic subdivisions that have the same common denominator, played together at the same tempo to create a third melody.

Cuíca or "kuweeca": A Brazilian friction drum with a large pitch range, produced by changing tension on the head of the drum. It is most often used in Samba music. The tone it produces has a high-pitched squeaky timbre. It has been called a "laughing gourd."

Djembe: A goblet-shaped wooden drum originating from the Malinke people in West Africa and played by hand.

Event: In this book it is defined as a beat that you can hear on the drum.

Fanga: *Fanga* is a rhythm from Liberia, both a dance and a song introduced in this country by Pearl Primus, dance pioneer. The dance, rhythm and song were taught by Baba Olatunji at his workshops and classes.

Ga Ma La: *TaKeTiNa* rhythm syllables developed by Reinhard Flatischler which indicate the rhythmic structure of three: *Ga* = one, *Ma* = two and *La* = three.

Gun, go do, pa ta: (*Gun* pronounced *goon*) Baba Olatunji's drum language. *Gun* is the bass note, *go* and *do* are the tones, and *pa* and *ta* are the slaps or high notes.

Kpanlogo: (The *k* is silent. Say "*pan-logo*.") A recreational dance and music form from Ghana, West Africa. It was first played by the *Ga* ethnic group, most of whom live in and around the capital city, Accra, but is now performed and enjoyed throughout the country.

Measure: In musical notation, a bar (or measure) is a segment of time corresponding to a specific number of beats in which each beat is represented by a particular note value and the boundaries of the bar are indicated by vertical bar lines.

Motif: Two (or more) notes side by side; a musical fragment.

Ngoma: Musical instruments used by certain Bantu-speaking peoples of Africa; *ngoma* is, simply, the Kongo word for "drum."

Orchestration: Different accompaniments that when played together make up a specific rhythm and melody for a drum group.

Pandeiro: A type of hand-held frame drum with a round wooden frame and six pairs of metal discs fit along the sides, and an animal skin or nylon head; similar to a tambourine but with head tension that can be tuned to make crisper, drier, and less sustained jingles, used in a number of Brazilian music forms.

Polyrhythm: See Cross Rhythm above.

Reggae, Ska and Soul: All three are different genres of music. Reggae and Ska came from Jamaica and originated from the Calypso and Mento music of the Caribbean. All three musical genres share the same emphasis on the second and fourth beats of a 4/4 tune.

Rhythmic structure: Groupings of rhythms that inform movement on the drum and in the body.

Samba: A Brazilian musical genre and dance style originating in Brazil, with its roots in Africa via the West African slave trade and African religious traditions, particularly Angola and the Congo.

Surdo: A large bass drum used in many kinds of Brazilian music, such as Axé/Samba-reggae and samba, where it plays the lower parts from a percussion section.

TaKeTiNa **musical notation:** Vocables or rhythmic syllables that indicate how a rhythmic structure is divided into beats. For example, *Ta* and *Ki* are used as 1 and 2 in a two-beat subdivision. *Ga Ma La* indicates the subdivision of three; *Ga* is one, *Ma* is two and *La* is three. *Ta Ke Ti Na* indicates four, and so on.

Tempo: The speed at which music is played.

Training Wheels: A *TaKeTiNa* step pattern in 4/4 time, in which the steps are on the *Ta* and *Ti* (the 1 and 3).

Top part: Usually indicates the higher, more complex parts in a drum orchestration.

Unit box notation: A system for writing out rhythms, similar to traditional musical notation. It is particularly useful to show the different parts that add up to a complex rhythmic texture. It is also important to see the spaces or intervals between the notes/events.

Vocables: Rhythm syllables—not words, just voiced syllables like *TaKeTiNa* or even *lalala* that can be used to count out rhythms.

Resources

Here are a few resources for those of you yearning for more than your weekly classes. There are many ways to go into a group experience to learn more about drumming and percussion and to experience a little of the feeling of village life.

Twenty-five years ago, when I began drumming, I lived for my March and July week-long workshops with Baba. I would call the Esalen office and register for the workshop as soon as the catalog came in the mail. Getting to be around Baba for a week of rhythmic bliss, I was returning home to my adult playground, bathed in the awesome physical beauty of Esalen besides! There were lots of other camps as well—some I participated in and others that came highly recommended. (And these are only the ones on this coast!)

Drum Camps

Congo Camp, founded by the late Malonga Casquelourd, is held near Ukiah, CA. Around two hundred drummers and dancers show up for a weeklong immersion in Congolese music, including *mbira* (thumb piano), songs, drum, dance, performance, and food! The teachers are amazing. They teach about the culture. They ARE the culture. The camp is like a mini-hit of life on the African continent. It is a wonderful opportunity to hang out with the Congolese family in the US. Kids are welcome. Check out the youth programs! There's also a Congolese winter program every year in Hawaii.

Camp Fareta, West African Drum and Dance Camp may be sponsored by various organizations; Kumandi and Tambacounda Productions are two of the top ones. All are versions of the expression of Guinean, Senegalese, and Malian West African arts, with exceptional artists: drummers, dancers, singers, and performers on the kora (a harp-like instrument) and other instruments.

There is also an incredible **California Brazilian Camp** for all arts Brazilian, including *samba*, *bateria*, vocals, dance, and *capoeira* classes. World-renowned drum, dance, and song teachers Jorge Albe, Jorjao Oliveira, and Michael Spiro, to name a few of the luminaries.

You can go to a Zimbabwe camp for marimba playing (**Zimfest** is one).

The Lark in the Morning's **Lark Camp** gives you a taste of different percussion and musical styles and dances from around the world.

Women's Drum Camp—Born to Drum. The most wonderful women teachers! Many of the teachers are from the Bay Area: Carolyn Brandy, Afia Walking Tree, and some others from past camps are Edwina Tyler, Mabiba Baegne, Virginia Lopez, Ubaka Hill and Barbara Borden.

Arthur Hull's week-long **Hawaii Drum Circle Facilitator's Training** dives deep into how to effectively lead drum circles. You also get to hang out with some amazing people who are leading circles all over the world.

Schools

You can go the more traditional route of Western academia and enroll in a program in **Ethnomusicology**. Most are Masters or Doctorate programs—very small enrollment and often connected to sociology or cultural anthropology. There are a good many schools to choose from, including Harvard, Columbia, Oxford, the University of Hawaii, and California Institute of the Arts (CalArts).

In an ethnomusicology program you will learn about all kinds of cultural musical expression, not just African drumming, such as *gamelan* orchestra from Java and Bali or *Samulnori* from Korea. You can choose to go to Africa and study at the **International Centre for African Music and Dance** at the University of Accra in Legon, Ghana, where you learn the indigenous dance, songs and music of all Ghanaian ethnic groups (tribes) and the surrounding area. The possibilities are endless. Cameron Tummel, for example, is an excellent drummer, teacher, and drum circle facilitator who studied with Arthur Hull and Abdoulaye Diakité, traveled to Senegal for further learning, then continued his journey into the academic world and recently completed his master's degree in world percussion at CalArts.

In a non-Western-academic, but specific traditional way, you can join a **Tam Tam Mandingue (TTM®)**—a curriculum of West African music on and *dununb*a passed on by **Mamedy Keita**, one of the greatest drummers and also a heck of a GREAT teacher. There are TTM teachers all over the world, and most notably in the US in Chicago, Washington DC, Winston-Salem NC, and Santa Cruz and San Diego, CA.

You can become a TTM "professor," a teacher or assistant teacher, learning and being able to retain many different rhythms of the complete repertoire of music representing the Guinean/Malian/Senegalese culture. It is fascinating how many people are specifically studying this type of drumming, especially when they are not African at all, except remotely through their DNA.

Wild Encounters

Last but not least, I need to mention two other forms of drum encounters:

Fire Tribes: I went to the **Phoenix Fire** gathering a few years back in the Santa Cruz Mountains. The event seems like a cross between hard-core drummers and earth-based pagan and druidic sorts, spoken-word aficionados and lovers of ritual and magick. It was wonderful.

After some preparation you drum all night long…the fire burning throughout the night as well. The experience was profound. The power of the ongoing rhythm takes one over into a sense of tribal belonging that is deeply satisfying. At three o'clock in the morning the crowd thins out and everything becomes more sensitive. You hear the softer percussion as well as *didgeridus*, flutes and *berimbaus*. Magic time.

Burning Man: I haven't yet been to **Burning Man**, but I know there is a drum camp and many, many opportunities to play. One of my friends has constructed a way to play his *surdo* drum while on stilts…he's been there…so there's room for everything!

Acknowledgements and Thanks

To My Teachers
and Board of Advisors

Blessings, thanks and praises. Without your encouragement, teaching and friendship there wouldn't be a book. All of you are and have been important in my development as a drummer, dancer, and lover of rhythm. Thank you for what you have given me to pass on to others.

Baba Olatunji

What more can I say? I was not the only one touched by the magic that moved through Baba. But there were some things he did or said at times that were downright eerie, as if he was reading my mind. I would tell him I was struggling with something—my feelings about my relationships with other drummers, or a conundrum I was struggling with. One time in the middle of class he stopped what we were doing and started telling a story that seemed to be going nowhere. Out of this meandering tale he said (and I swear it was for me and me alone), "Instead of getting angry or hurt or bothered by what someone is doing, just blink them out."

When Baba died, I lost not only my teacher, but an important spiritual mentor who always put the problems in my life in perspective. He got me to lighten up. He would say, "There are no problems, only situations that need to be resolved."

Sanga of the Valley

Trickster, prankster, great drummer, amazing teacher, lover of women and the ganja. Mr Rasta.

Sanga is well versed as a drummer, and was often Baba's lead drummer on his teaching tours at Esalen. Even more than his skill as a drummer, he knows how to teach. He understands ways to illuminate good technique, how to make your sounds, *Gun, go do* and *pa*, credible and reliable. His clear teaching creates a map for you to find those places on the drum again and again. He makes you laugh, and rhythm just begins to move through you.

I had one specially magical moment with Sanga. We were in a workshop together and he said, "Zorina, play Maculele." Consciously, I did not remember the rhythm worth a damn. After my initial panic, I relaxed—and lo and behold, my hands started playing the rhythm. Nothing in my mind was telling me anything! My body remembered it all. It was another moment that reminded me that there is more than the conscious mind involved in learning rhythms.

When you play with Sanga, you get his philosophy, which is funny, irreverent, honest, and sideways spiritual. I am so tickled to have him as an influence and teacher.

Yao Tamakloe

Yao had an American name also: **Ronnie Marshall**. Yao was an African prince and a homeboy all in one. From his Chicago roots, he said, he was headed for a gangsta life. His aunt picked him up off the street and put him in tap dancing classes. From then on, dance more than street life was his focus. (There was basketball too….)

He took his name Tamakloe from a family that "adopted" him when he went to study dance in Ghana for seven years. Yao is a traditional Ghanaian name for boy children born on Thursday.

When I met Yao he was Baba's dance teacher at Esalen (although he could play drum pretty well too!). We both had young boys around the same age and our sons hung out together. (His wife, Anindo Marshall, is a talented singer and dancer in her own right. She currently plays in a kick-ass Adduwa all-female percussion group in Los Angeles.)

I got flak from some of my fellow students when I started to teach. Yao said, "Well, what is it that they are doing? People are always willing to criticize others when they aren't doing anything themselves." It was great to feel his support.

Arthur Hull

My drum brother, Arthur. When I met Arthur he was teaching drum classes on the beach in Santa Cruz, his hometown. We were both greatly influenced by Baba, although Arthur had been a drummer for a long time and I was just new to it. Arthur, recognized as the father of the Drum Circle Facilitator Movement, was manufacturing his own drums, Village Music Drums. He sold his design to Remo drums in the late eighties, and has been touring the world as Johnny Drumseed ever since.

When I got my first drumming group teaching gig for a women's conference, I drove to Arthur's home in Santa Cruz and borrowed thirty drums from him! He has mentored me around drum politics, held my hand during transitions of power, followed my development, and still does. He is on my Board of Advisors. He has always been there to support and contribute, and if need be, kick me in the ass. He is a take-no-prisoners-because-we-are-going-to-turn-them-into-participants kind of guy!

In 2009 I went to Arthur's Hawaii Drum Facilitators Training. I had such a great time. And I learned so much about effective guiding of a drum circle. I count myself a lucky person to be part of Arthur's family. Drum Circle Facilitators rock!

Sikiru Adepoju

Sikiru was another member of Baba's band—the talking drum player, an accomplished musician in his own right. Currently he is a drummer in Mickey Hart's band, Rhythm Devils. When he was with Baba, he was in the background. But he was actually running things and making all transactions as smooth as possible for Baba and the Drums of Passion band. We both agree that even though Baba has passed on, we are still working for him.

Here are two Sikiru stories:

On my birthday, a year after I began drumming, I invited some friends to come over, and invited Sikiru to come and teach. For organizing the class, Sikiru was going to give me a private lesson. At the end of the day, everyone left, and finally I was about to have my private lesson. Sikiru said, "Play Baba's rhythmic pattern number six, which goes: *Gun go do go do Gun pa go pa go.*

I played it the best I could as a beginner—probably no slaps and erratic tempo—and Sikiru said, "Okay, I'll see you next year." Message: *Now work on this so I actually have something to teach you.*

The second time I came to Esalen for the seven-day Baba workshop I noticed that everything I did, whether it was walking or talking or eating or rolling around in bed, had this rhythmic component to it. I went to sleep in rhythm, I woke up in rhythm. I went to Sikiru and said, "What is happening? All I hear in every moment is rhythm!" He smiled, and said, "Now you have entered reality! This is the way life naturally is!"

Ma Boukaka

Ma Boukaka was the kind of teacher that you had to hang out with to get. I was lucky to have had some time with him, and to be recognized by him.

I knew Ma Boukaka from the first, and always felt his friendly vibe. We put on a gig together at the Masonic Temple, a drum circle followed by Bole Bantu, his band. They played. We danced. Very good vibes. I liked him. He had these funny, sparkly, electric-lighted sunglasses. He was his own person.

When I met Baba Olatunji, I was bitten by the African drumming and dance bug. I needed to

Baba's Rhythmic Pattern Number 6											
Ga	Ma	La	Ga	Ma	La	Ga	Ma	La	Ga	Ma	La
1	2	3	1	2	3	1	2	3	1	2	3
Gun		go	do	go	do	Gun	pa	go	pa	go	

study with someone in between the times that I saw Baba (every six months or so). I began with Fred Simpson, local teacher and Congolese drummer (also West African). Fred's classes were hard in lots of ways—not easy for me to learn. Felt dumb, dumb, dumb. Competition high, competence low.

Went to lots (years) of other classes too before I just broke. Said to myself, "This is not fun. I feel bad about myself." No warm fuzzies. No encouragement, no nurturing, just vying to be either fastest, loudest, quickest to learn rhythms, or most athletic. Had nothing to do with the spirit that drew me to drumming in the first place. (Even with Baba the stakes were high. People were angry at me for taking my seat next to the Man. Little did they know how much the seat cost.)

By the time I got to Ma Boukaka's classes I was more than a little sore from the drum community and its lack of cooperative spirit. Remember, there were very, very few women drummers at that time. The women who were serious about it were as bad if not worse than the men in their lack of generous-hearted inclusion. They had to have even more testosterone than the guys, and had much more to prove. Do I sound like I'm whining? I am not. It was what happened. It was a hard seven or so years for me. After one particularly harsh teacher in Oakland, I retreated with my tail between my legs, my sense of self-esteem in the toilet, and my hope to get any better as a drummer pretty dim.

But there was also this drive that would not let me give up—rhythm that calls. The calling for mastery, passion. So many things. A calling.

So, after playing with the big boys felt worse and worse, I gave up Fred (and others). And I started going to Boukaka's class, Tuesday nights, at Peninsula School, Menlo Park, CA. Now I was also learning the *ngoma* or conga, with different techniques (closed slap, muffled slaps), although the sensibility of singing and playing together was still the same as *djembe*.

Boukaka was from the Bantu tribe in the Congo. According to the stories he told, he was originally a safari guide and cook for white folks who were roughing it in the jungles of the Congo. By some strange set of circumstances, he arrived in the U.S. in the early sixties and landed on the San Francisco Bay Peninsula.

When you went to class with Ma Boukaka there was no ego, no hierarchical structure. You were taught village style. It was more like hanging out with the village elder. You just hung out week after week while he covered some of the same rhythms. In time, you got them. There was no real breaking down of anything. There were always songs and stories, mostly about roosters or women kicking their men out for drinking too much. Stuff like that. Little by little you learned about the culture.

Ma Boukaka had all sorts of chants and endless numbers of rhythms. He would point to me (or someone else in the class) and say, "Zorina, you play this…." He would play that part for a minute until I got it, and then go on to the next person and say, "Brad, you play this," etc. Eventually everyone got in. As the class continued, we got onto the next rhythm and played it for a half hour or so. Sometimes the music sounded amazing. And sometimes it never got off the ground. This style of learning and low-key-ness was a real rest from the aggression that I had been experiencing in Oakland and Santa Cruz.

I really appreciated (and still do) the easy way the class was taught, and Ma Boukaka's egalitarian quality. What a balm.

Some people like Geoff, Judy, Bob, and Brad were there since God, and the class was always mixed levels. Anthony was there a lot, too—very good drummer. Some guy used to come in and wait for class to be done so he could play piano. It was very casual and just what I needed. I felt included and less defensive.

I went to Congo camp with the Congolese family because of Ma Boukaka's inclusive vibe.

And there were others who were great people to meet. Nancy, Ma Boukaka's wife—good dancer, fine person. Regine, Ma Boukaka's daughter, great dance teacher. Malonga Casquelourd, Titos Sompa, Mbembe, Matingou, Samba Ngo, Mabiba Baegne and others. Hundreds of dancers. Lots and lots of drummers, from beginners to professionals. Long enough to sink into the vibe of being. Singing, *kalimba*, camping, paddling on the little pond. And Ma Boukaka in the kitchen—in a way, holding the whole thing together.

Boukaka's *Bole Bantu* played great dance music for my 50th birthday celebration, and for Terry's and my wedding.

What is it that makes a great teacher for a student? I think it is when you are recognized—not for what you can do in the moment, but for your *potential*, the thing that makes you unique. It is not egoic. It is about knowing inside that your contribution is important to the whole.

Everyone needs to be validated. Yes, you have to do your own work and lick your wounds, do your forgiving, put the past in a sensible light. But when someone you honor honors you back, your progress on this path of self-healing can advance by leaps and bounds. That is what Mr. Thomas Boukaka gave to me: encouragement, faith, hope.

Thank you, Ma Boukaka—for everything.

Mestre Beicola

Close to the time I was beginning my first *TaKeTiNa* training, I took some private lessons with Mestre Beicola, a *capoeira* master from Brazil. *Capoeira* is a martial art form and dance that came out of Brazil during the time of the slave trade. It was actually a very clever way for the slaves to practice the skills necessary to mount a revolution, while looking like they were executing dance moves.

Beicola is a kind man and a good teacher. I would come to his house for a lesson and get fed in many ways, through his patience as well as the goodies that he offered. Although I didn't get to study with him for long, his sensitivity to how I was learning really impressed me. Whenever I got too tense, a tea break would just happen to happen. It was designed to break the tension of the learning. He understood intuitively that you couldn't put anything into a container that was already full.

Val Serrant

I mention Val, another member of Baba's band, even though he was not formally my teacher. I don't know if he was aware of it or not, but he was an ally in my learning. One day we were in Huxley meeting space at Esalen, and we started to play a rhythm together. This might sound funny, but that was a thrill in itself. At Baba's workshop, I rarely got a chance to play with any of his drummers. I felt like the kid sister hanging around my big brothers, hoping that they'd throw me a crumb. So there Val and I were playing, and slowly, he began to speed up the rhythm, and speed it up, and speed it up, until I was just hanging on by my fingertips, with my hair blowing out behind me in the breeze. Heavy breathing on my part and I just hung out. Finally the space ship came down from the stratosphere and landed. Someone came into the room at that moment and asked what we were doing, and Val looked up with a twinkle in his eye, and said, "We were just taking Zorina out for a little ride." What a lovely ride. What a great guy.

Reinhard Flatischler

Despite the fact that I have ended my relationship with this teacher, I would be remiss not to mention Reinhard Flatischler. He is founder of *TaKeTiNa*, a brilliant body of work. I had the good fortune to study intensively with Reinhard and his (then) wife, Cornelia, for ten full years. The *TaKeTiNa* rhythm method allows anyone, whether musically trained or not, to enter into complex rhythm information in an intuitive, nonlinear way. The body is the primary instrument: footsteps, clapping, and voice. I am deeply grateful that Reinhard and Cornelia and I worked together to make this teaching available in the United States.

Alalade Dreamer Frederick

Alalade is the only one mentioned here who is not my drum teacher per se. She is a wonderfully skilled dance teacher, and was Baba's dance captain on his teaching tours and his troupe for many years. When you took a class with Baba, you learned all the aspects of the African arts, drum, dance, and song. For drummers, it is important to understand how the rhythms feel in the body. Alalade would break down the movements so even the klutziest dancer could find their way into dancing to the drum. She was a touchstone for me to learn all the movements to a dance, and she understood the spirituality within this form. And even though she was my teacher, we were both students of Baba. Thank you, my East Coast sister, for your teaching, your friendship and our journey together.

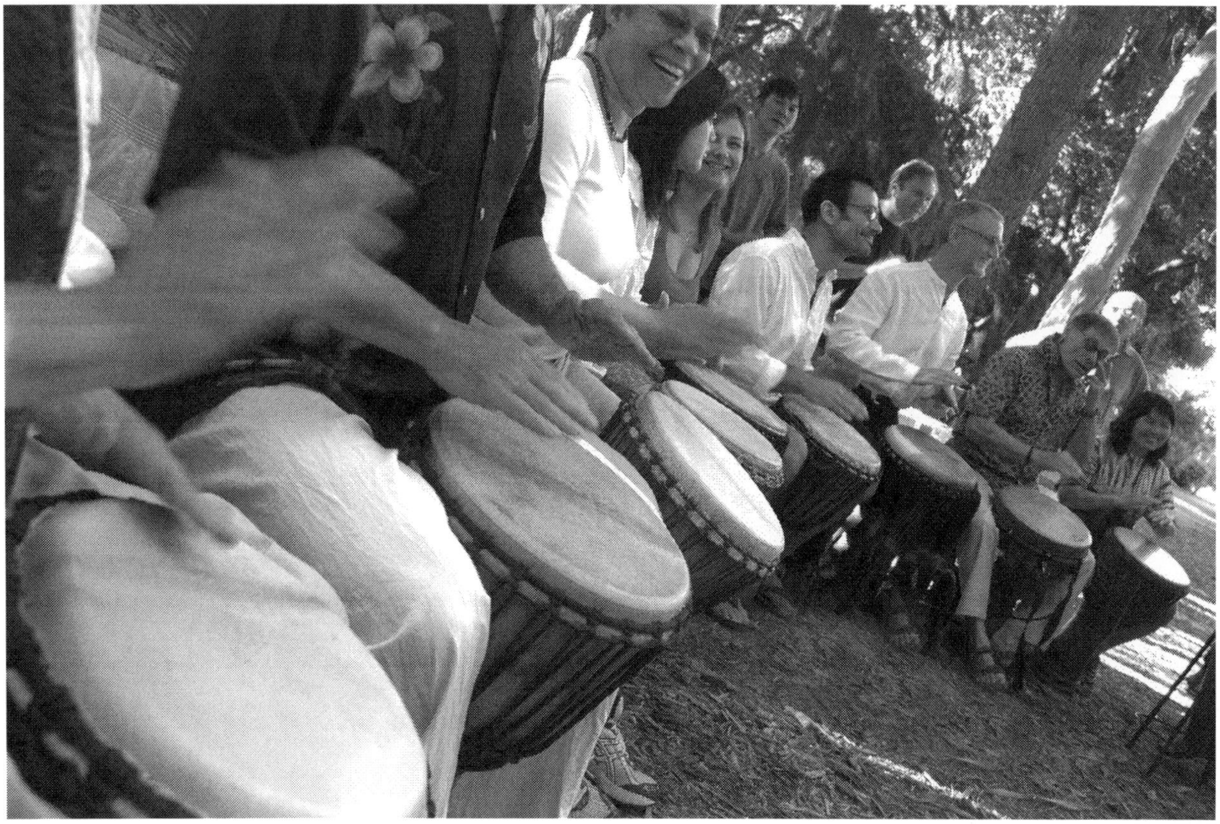

Made in the USA
Middletown, DE
03 August 2020